The Money Tree

PEARSON
Prentice Hall
BUSINESS

Books that make you better

Books that make you better. That make you *be* better, *do* better, *feel* better. Whether you want to upgrade your personal skills or change your job, whether you want to improve your managerial style, become a more powerful communicator, or be stimulated and inspired as you work.

Prentice Hall Business is leading the field with a new breed of skills, careers and development books. Books that are a cut above the mainstream – in topic, content and delivery – with an edge and verve that will make you better, with less effort.

Books that are as sharp and smart as you are.

Prentice Hall Business.
We work harder – so you don't have to.

For more details on products, and to contact us, visit
www.pearsoned.co.uk

The Money Tree

Money. How to make it, save it
and grow it.

Martin Bamford

PEARSON
Prentice Hall
BUSINESS

Harlow, England • London • New York • Boston • San Francisco • Toronto • Sydney • Singapore • Hong Kong
Tokyo • Seoul • Taipei • New Delhi • Cape Town • Madrid • Mexico City • Amsterdam • Munich • Paris • Milan

PEARSON EDUCATION LIMITED

Edinburgh Gate
Harlow CM20 2JE
Tel: +44 (0)1279 623623
Fax: +44 (0)1279 431059

Website: www.pearsoned.co.uk

First published in Great Britain in 2006

© Informed Choice Ltd 2006

ISBN-13: 978-0-273-70834-6
ISBN-10: 0-273-70834-1

British Library Cataloguing-in-Publication Data
A catalogue record for this book can be obtained from the British Library

Library of Congress Cataloging-in-Publication Data
Bamford, Martin.
   The money tree : Money. How to make it, save it and grow it.
  / Martin Bamford.
     p. cm.
   Includes index.
   ISBN-13: 978-0-273-70834-6 (alk. paper)
   ISBN-10: 0-273-70834-1 (alk. paper)
    1. Finance, Personal. I. Title.

HG179.B288 2006
332.024'01—dc22

2006049546

10 9 8 7 6 5 4 3 2 1
10 09 08 07 06

Designed by designdeluxe
Typeset in 10pt Iowan Old Style by 70
Printed and bound by Bell & Bain Limited, Glasgow

The Publisher's policy is to use paper manufactured from sustainable forests.

About the author

Martin Bamford is an independent financial adviser and director of professional advisory firm Informed Choice Ltd. At only 27 years old he already holds the Advanced Financial Planning Certificate from the Chartered Insurance Institute (CII). On a daily basis Martin and his firm give advice and wisdom to a wide range of clients – from plumbers to lords of the realm.

Martin is an associate of the Personal Financial Society and an associate of the Institute of Financial Planning. He is no stranger to the media, writing for *Investment Week* and regularly quoted in the national press, including the *Telegraph*, the *Observer*, *The Times* and the *Independent*.

In his capacity as a financial expert, Martin is a regular guest on the Anna Raeburn show on London's LBC Radio 97.3FM.

Martin leads independent financial advisers when it comes to innovation. In September 2005 he produced the first ever personal finance podcast from an IFA which is now highly rated on leading podcast directory iTunes. His firm was nominated at the Money Marketing Financial Services Awards 2006 for the Innovation in Distribution award.

In addition to his work as an IFA, with both private and corporate clients, Martin is a prolific networker. He is one of the most connected people on Ecademy.com, the social business networking platform.

Martin lives in Surrey with his wife, Lindie, and their Labrador, Rufus. In his spare time Martin enjoys walking in the countryside, scuba-diving and fly-fishing.

Thank you

(In no particular order) thank you for helping me put this book together, helping me get to where I am today and teaching me a thing or two about growing a Money Tree:

Rachael Stock and all at Prentice Hall, Clare Christian at The Friday Project, everybody I have talked to and met from Ecademy.com, Clare Evans, Phil Calvert, David Scarlett, Jon Riley, Jonny Restrick, Edward Steiger, Wendy Stephens, Michelle Whittick, Ewan MacLeod, Nick Ris, Nick and Andy, Emma, Sandy Lowth, Philip Sullivan, Martin Barkwill, Andrew Newman, Tony Wynne, Christine Morris, Terry O'Neill, Sarah Calvert, Amanda Newman, Leonora Walters, Anna Raeburn, Melanie Wright, Ray Morrison, and (most importantly) Lindie – for putting up with me when I act like a hermit and providing an endless supply of cups of tea!

Contents

CHAPTER 03

Serious about savings 55

CHAPTER 04

Making the most of your mortgage 74

Plan to protect 97

Intelligent investment 114

A financially secure retirement 139

Time for advice 160

Bringing it all together 179

Introduction

> Money, if it does not bring you happiness, will at least help you be miserable in comfort.
>
> Helen Gurley Brown (1922–)

An old proverb tells us that money doesn't grow on trees. Well, not literally of course. But while money might not be easy to come by, and it certainly isn't easy to hold on to, I believe it *is* possible to grow your own Money Tree. Not only possible, but maybe also easier than you think.

Taking charge of your financial situation may not be something you relish the thought of – however, it is well worth your while. In fact it could transform your life. Money is important. When you feel confident about your financial decisions, you'll probably find you sleep a lot easier at night. When you feel unsure about your money situation it can weigh on your mind until you take the decisive action needed to fix the problem.

Reading this book will take away a lot of pressure and give you peace of mind as well as a more prosperous future. Money might not be the *most* important thing in life, but a lack of it, or a lack of control over it, can affect our whole lives, including our mental and physical health. Nobody enjoys life when they are out of control financially. Simply put, *The Money Tree* will make your life easier.

Yet so many people neglect their own Money Tree. Some choose to bury their head in the sand. Through lack of time, inclination, or a combination of the two, this sometimes feels like the easy option. Fear of putting in some effort to master our finances can hold us back. The 'ostrich' option, avoiding having to tackle the issue of money head on, seems far easier than taking action. But it's no solution. A little knowledge and understanding can take away the fear – and it doesn't have to be painful or boring. In fact it can be uplifting and liberating! The basics of money are not difficult to grasp. Anyone can grow a strong and healthy Money Tree. It doesn't take much in the way of brains, simply a desire to be in charge of and understand what is going on in your purse or wallet.

It's time to take a really positive step. You have already made one positive step by buying this book. The second step? Reading it! If you are feeling really brave then you can take the third positive step towards growing your Money Tree – start to put some of the ideas here into action and enjoy a life with lower levels of financial stress now and greater prosperity in the future.

The purpose of this book

I want to capture your imagination and show you what is possible when you take control of your money.

Personal finance doesn't need to be dull. It's only boring if you don't understand it or if you don't want to understand it. Start to appreciate the mechanics of money and all of a sudden you will open your eyes to a world of wealth and financial opportunities.

The complexity that is sometimes associated with personal financial planning is, unfortunately, unavoidable. However, it *is* something that is manageable. Changing your attitude towards money is the first step in understanding what is possible and what you should avoid.

In my line of work there is nothing worse than meeting someone who has been a 'sales victim' in the past. They come to see me with carrier bags full of financial paperwork that relates to products they simply don't need and certainly don't understand.

If *The Money Tree* stops you from becoming a sales victim in the future and helps you to start asking the right questions when it comes to your personal financial planning then I will have met my aims and will sleep well. I hope that you will be able to as well.

What will this book do for you?

When it comes to your own financial planning there are no clear-cut right or wrong answers. This book acts as a valuable source of information and also a toolkit for developing your understanding of all the important money-related areas, including savings, mortgages, protection, investments, debt, tax and retirement planning. It is intended to complement the services of a professional adviser rather than replace them. It will enable you to take some important actions on your own, but as your individual circumstances, goals and objectives have a key role in deciding on the best money strategy for you personally, it can't give you all the answers. However, when you do need specific advice, having read this book you will be in a much stronger position to challenge, question and understand an adviser.

I firmly believe that all of my own clients already hold all of the answers. They sometimes lack product-specific knowledge or a detailed understanding of tax, legislation or processes required to grow their Money Tree. My role is that of facilitator; someone to assist with finding these hidden solutions. It is my aim to help create a clear vision of the most suitable way to a prosperous financial future.

This book is designed to provide a solid framework for growing your own Money Tree. It is not, however, intended to be a comprehensive source of information. Financial planning is, by its very nature, a complex beast. However, getting to grips with the key elements that make up the art of financial planning will help you on the road towards financial security.

Taking financial control

The financial decisions you make during your life will often be new, exciting and, more often than not, quite daunting.

It's no wonder that financial choices we have to take are so bewildering. Financial planning is not a subject widely taught in schools. The media frequently bombards us with horror stories of ripped-off consumers, misselling scandals and failed investments. Debt is offered (even encouraged) from the moment we start work until (and sometimes after) the day we retire.

Our parents are often the main source of our own financial education. For many years during our childhoods they control our main source of income – our pocket-money and allowances! They can also have a massive influence over our spending and saving habits as we grow up. During this time our attitudes towards money are formed.

But money may have become a taboo subject in polite company. At best we manage to get to grips with money in small stages: we might receive a bit of advice from an accountant or be sold a financial product from a financial adviser or bank. Then a solicitor might tidy up the mess when we eventually die and our estate is passed to our children. This approach does not make for a happy life or a positive relationship with money!

The system of financial advice in this country is partly to blame for this personal financial crisis. Financial sales are often wrongly labelled as financial advice which leads to a culture of mistrust. It has been difficult for most people to establish a trusted and long-term relationship with their financial adviser against this backdrop of misselling and commission bias on product selection.

I will give you the information that will enable you to take back control of your money, make some decisions for yourself and, where you need to seek financial advice, to do so from a position of confidence that will allow you to work with your financial adviser, as partners, where you have control.

The Money Tree rule book

There are six financial rules that everyone who wants to grow a Money Tree should live by. The following points are not rocket science but fundamental principles that will help you form a solid base for understanding the concepts to be discussed.

1 Spend less than you earn

A really simple concept, but it still surprises me that people cannot accept this is the best way to handle their money. Mr Micawber in Charles Dickens's *David Copperfield* sums this up nicely:

> Annual income twenty pounds, annual expenditure nineteen ninety-six, result happiness. Annual income twenty pounds, annual expenditure twenty pounds ought and six, result misery.

If your expenditure (the money that leaves your pocket each month) is more than your income (money in) you need to have a major overhaul not only of your lifestyle but also your attitude towards money. What are you spending money on that causes this unsustainable imbalance to occur?

If you earn £1,000 each month, make sure that you never spend more than £999. Change your mindset to understand that you do not have more than this to spend. If you are spending £1,001, you are spending somebody else's money, and they will want it back at some point (with interest!).

2 A tight budget is doomed to failure

While you need to make sure that you don't spend more than you earn each month, running a really tight budget rarely works for long. If you budget to spend every last penny of your salary each month you are planning for a disaster. It will only take one unexpected item of expenditure to screw up your plans. A car breakdown or some emergency dental work will throw you off course and it will take you a long time to get back on to the right track.

The people I meet who have very tight budgets constantly worry about their money. They feel that they need to account for every penny and this leads to anxiety. Money begins to control them when they should be controlling their money.

3 Never get a store card

If you need to use a store card to buy clothes or other items on the high street it means that you cannot afford them. Using store card credit is using someone else's money to get the things you want. It also ties you into buying goods from one shop (or group of shops) which prevents you from shopping around to get the best deal.

We will take a closer look at store cards on p. 21.

4 It costs more to borrow than you get paid to save

This is another principle examined in more detail on p. 23. The rate of interest on offer when you save money is always less than the rate you are charged to borrow money. This means that if you have £1,000 in savings and £1,000 in debt, the debt will cost you more than you can earn in interest from your savings. A further kick in the teeth – you get taxed on the savings interest (unless you use a cash ISA, as I explain in Chapter 06!).

I still discover new clients who are laden with short-term debt but have savings as well. They are working hard to save but this is a constant uphill struggle due to the dragging effect of the higher cost of the debt. It doesn't make sense yet it provides them with a comfort factor.

A simple rule: clear your short-term debt and only then start saving.

5 Never bury your head in the sand

Unopened credit card statements and unanswered letters from a bank manager are both signs of someone who is ignoring their current financial position in the irrational hope it will go away.

If you want a Money Tree you have to face up to the reality of your situation. When you have done it once, you have to do it on a regular basis. You need to know what your current financial position is. Don't become obsessive over the fine detail of the figures, but always keep on top of the broad numbers.

Ensure that your records are up to date and well organized. The simplest way of doing this is to invest a couple of quid in an A4 ring binder. Divide the binder into sections for different accounts and bills. Keep everything in one place in an ordered and tidy fashion.

6 If you live for today you will eventually wake up and realize it is tomorrow

Living for today is great fun. You get to spend what you have and make the most of every minute. Until tomorrow comes. Having this view of life and your finances only works over the very short term. Fortunately, the medium and long terms are also very real concerns for most of us.

The worst excuse I hear when it comes to saving money is, 'but I could get hit by a bus tomorrow' or 'I can't take my money with me when I die'. These people are right on both counts. But they are going to feel stupid when they run out of money and haven't put anything aside to deal with the future.

Most of us will lead long and healthy lives. Planning for this makes much better sense than planning for an early death.

The way we grow a Money Tree has changed

The concept of a job for life is well and truly out of the window for most people. No longer do most of us leave school, walk straight into the arms of an established local employer and happily complete fifty years of loyal service. Chopping and changing jobs in the name of career (and salary) progression has become the norm rather than the exception.

In fact, if the current trend continues, the concept of the employer may also be on the decline. There could well be a greater number of self-employed workers with less reliance on large companies for their careers in the next decades.

These changes to the typical working lifestyle will have a massive impact on managing your money. Traditionally, your long-term financial objectives would be closely linked to the consistency of your employment. As time went by your salary would increase (often due more to loyalty and length of service than the demonstration of any other discernible qualities). The company final salary pension would form the lynchpin of your long-term retirement planning. If you stayed in one job for long enough you could expect to retire on a healthy pension of two-thirds of your salary.

Now, as job change happens much more often, and especially when you are self-employed, it's vital that you take individual responsibility when it comes to your money.

A long-term career with a single employer can lead to healthy employee and retirement benefits. A lifetime of various short-term employment contracts will have the effect of a complex and fragmented collection of policies and entitlements to benefits.

Taking individual responsibility for your Money Tree in this new landscape means three main things:

- Taking responsibility to understand. You have already taken a major step towards improving your financial literacy by starting to read this book. By the time you have finished it you will have a better understanding of the financial aspects of your life than most of the people you know (unless you happen to know a lot of financial advisers, accountants and stockbrokers!).
- Your financial education doesn't end with reading this book. To truly understand what it takes to manage your money you have to get your hands dirty. Really start to dig into the money matters that have the biggest impact on your life. Take the time out to read (and question) the statements from your bank, building society and mortgage lender.
- Take decisive action, now! It is a simple fact of life that any form of saving or investment has the potential to be worth more the earlier you start. The younger you are and the earlier you start, the better your chance of getting a head start on your future financial planning.

But just how do you measure success when it comes to growing your Money Tree? In my time working as a financial adviser I've discovered that one method that is commonly used is the position on pay-day each month.

If you can actually get to pay-day with some money left over from the month before then you are doing something right! This is a very simple measure but it certainly beats being in a position where you start each month with a deficit.

Starting the month in debt puts you on the back foot from day one. You are playing catch-up straight away and this makes it more difficult to get to the start of the next month with cash in your pocket.

Getting yourself into the position where you are receiving your pay cheque and not having to allocate a proportion of it (and in some cases a significant proportion of it) to funding the excesses of your lifestyle in the previous month certainly is an indication that you are pretty good with your money.

Before you get too smug and think, 'I manage this each month so I must be doing all right', bear in mind that this makes you reasonably good with your money, not brilliant. There's a way to go yet!

What works best for you?

No single system for managing finances will work for everyone. While there are a number of 'rules', these are financial common sense. The rest is best left to you as an individual to tailor. Find out what works for you.

For example, my wife and I both have different ways of reducing our own expenditure on unnecessary items. Lindie makes sure that she doesn't carry cash in her purse. If she doesn't have cash readily available then she won't buy small objects that she doesn't really need. Her mindset tells her that using plastic (either a debit or a credit card) is reserved for larger purchases like petrol or the weekly food shopping.

It's a completely different story with me. I always make sure that I have around £10 in my wallet or I find myself squandering loads of money on unnecessary small bits and pieces. I fail to make the mental connection between plastic and cash. When I use a debit or credit card to buy things it doesn't feel like I'm actually spending my money. The introduction of chip and pin has made this even worse for me! I don't even need to go through the very formal procedure of putting pen to paper any more to buy things. Just tapping in that four-digit code is enough to complete the transaction and leaves my bank account feeling a bit lighter each and every day.

What works best for you? Do you fritter away your money when your purse is empty and plastic is the only option, or does having a wad of notes in your wallet make it more likely that you will squander your hard-earned cash?

Different things work for different people. By starting to address and recognize your attitude towards money you are taking a positive step towards being in control of your relationship with it.

How to grow your Money Tree

I've tried to write this book in a way that will be easy to read but also rewarding. Each chapter covers a different part of the Money Tree and starts with the basics, moves on to more complex areas of that subject and finishes with advanced techniques for growing your Tree.

The roots

The depth and length of your Money Tree's roots are both essential features in its likely success (or failure). Deeper roots give you access to more information, knowledge and understanding. To have deep roots you have to read widely, take an active interest in your finances and talk to the right people. You should always aim to absorb financial knowledge whenever you are exposed to it, and you should do this on a regular basis. Just as a real tree needs water and nutrients to survive, grow and prosper, your Money Tree needs a regular supply of knowledge to do the same. The longer the roots are the more stable your Money Tree will be when times are tough. Only you can determine how deep and long the roots will be.

We will start by looking at one of the roots of the Money Tree – debt. Debt is a drag, and for many people it is a constant focus of their lives. We start with debt because you cannot grow a stable Money Tree until you have tackled any existing debt issues. I prefer to call debt an 'issue' rather than a 'problem' because some debt can be good debt. I truly believe that our attitude to debt can shape our attitude towards money in general. Some people live with debt their whole lives because they don't know what the alternative looks like or feels like.

After debt we move on to tax, another important root of the Money Tree. Understanding how tax works helps to form a cornerstone for our understanding of money. Tax is what is taken away from our earnings, savings interest and investment returns before we are left with money we can actually use. While the UK tax system is fairly rigid, it is still the case that many people pay more than they need to in taxes each year. The ability to legally 'avoid' tax and use careful planning to pay less tax where possible can lead to more money in your pocket and greater personal wealth. It is an important area to establish properly before moving on.

The final root of the Money Tree is savings. Establishing a strong savings culture will ensure that your Money Tree has a long and prosperous future. Savings is probably one of the most basic areas of financial planning, yet it is something people still manage to do badly. Getting your savings in shape will give your Tree some much needed stability and also give you the confidence to tackle the more complex areas of financial planning covered in Chapters 01–07.

The branches

There are four branches of the Money Tree: mortgages, protection, investments and retirement planning.

A mortgage is the biggest financial commitment you will ever have in your life. For many people it becomes the cause of stress and worry through misunderstanding. Mortgages are dead easy once you get to grips with the basics. Knowing how the different types of mortgages can work for you is the first step in taking control of your mortgage rather than letting it control you.

Protection is an unavoidable area of financial planning and something that we all have to address, even though it means dealing with a morbid subject. It is something we do because we feel a responsibility towards our loved ones. Yet protection can be a costly exercise. It can be difficult to establish what type and level of protection we need to put in place and this leaves many people with inadequate levels of cover. Chapter 05 will help you get your head round protection, the various options available, and how to work out exactly what it is you need.

Investing your money involves risk and people often misinterpret this risk before they make investment decisions. As well as explaining how investment works in the broadest sense I will also introduce you to my own strategy for investing money that moves making investment decisions away from luck. This will help you become an intelligent investor.

The final branch of the Money Tree is retirement planning. This is often a neglected area of financial planning because we don't get to experience the benefits of making sacrifices today for such a long time. It is always easy to push retirement planning aside when we have more pressing financial issues to deal with. As well as showing you some things you can do with a pension, Chapter 07 will also spur you into taking action over your retirement plans sooner rather than later.

With healthy roots and strong branches established you need to understand how to nurture and protect your Money Tree. The final two chapters on working with professional advisers and building your financial plan give you the tools you need to ensure your Money Tree continues to grow and also to make sure you avoid pests and disease.

Dealing with debt

> If I owe you a pound, I have a problem; but
> if I owe you a million, the problem is yours.
> John Maynard Keynes (1883–1946)

Debt to me represents two big issues:

1 It is a drag on your ability to save and to work towards other financial objectives.

2 It is mentally draining and poses a danger not only to your finances but also to your relationships, attitude and general well-being.

You only have to watch a bit of daytime television to see the plethora of advertisements offering debt management or consolidation services. As a nation we have a debt problem that is like an illness. We prefer to take on unsecured personal debt rather than wait a little while, save for an item and pay for it ourselves.

Even as an experienced and highly qualified financial adviser I'm not immune to the issues that surround debt. When I left full-time education, for a couple of years working in my first jobs I was laden with credit card debt. During this time I managed to convince myself that it really wasn't a problem. My earnings at the time were sufficient to repay the debt within a month or two if I wanted to. Buying things with the credit card was just easier at the time than worrying day to day about how much was sitting in my bank account or what I could actually 'afford' to buy.

My own foray into the murky world of credit cards worked out in the end. I finally made the decision that I wanted to be clear of unsecured debt. The prompt for me was wanting to take on my first mortgage to buy a swanky bachelor pad and move out of home! This meant suffering some financial hardship for five or six months while I redirected all of my spare cash to repaying the debt. It was a personal choice to spend less of my money on 'fun stuff' and have more spare income in the future.

It could have turned out differently. Once you burden yourself with unsecured debt it doesn't take much in the way of a change in circumstances to send you into a spiral of debt and financial depression. A sudden financial emergency or a reduction in earnings is usually all it takes. Meeting minimum payments on credit cards is a piece of cake when you have a predictable stream of income but all of a sudden becomes an impossible challenge if you lose your job.

Spot the sham

When I'm stuck in traffic on the way to see a client (or, more typically, on the way home afterwards) I play a game that I like to call 'spot the sham'. I'm getting quite good at this little game. It involves looking for expensive-looking cars that don't actually represent a show of wealth for the driver. What they are really sitting in (quickly going nowhere in the same traffic jam as me) is a flashy debt burden, and often a significant debt at that.

They might have a car that can go a little faster than mine. Perhaps the leather seats give them some additional comfort as the traffic edges forward another couple of metres. One thing is sure: we're both sitting in the same traffic jam but I own my car outright. The driver of 'the sham' is tied into making substantial monthly payments for a hunk of metal that is actually going down in value as the minutes fly past. It's expenditure that they are never going to recover. It is also the sort of debt that can often lead to bankruptcy if things in your life take an unexpected turn.

Now there is nothing wrong with owning and enjoying a nice car. If I could justify the cost then I would be the first to have something a bit faster, newer and shinier than my current vehicle. But I can't justify the expense right now. It's a monetary commitment that falls much lower down my list of financial priorities to even be a consideration at the moment.

This sort of thing really comes down to priorities. If you are single and love cars then having a flash motor might very well be your financial priority, and this is nothing to be ashamed of. For some it is cars and for others it might be expensive holidays or designer clothes. The method of reaching this priority is another matter. If the only way of achieving the goal is to sacrifice more important financial priorities then clearly something is wrong with your Money Tree and you need to take corrective action.

Getting into debt is really easy. Getting out of debt is much more of a challenge, as you may know. For some people debt just creeps up on them and before they realize it they have reached the bottom of a financial pit. Others may be aware of the increasing burden of their debt but feel either unable or unwilling to do anything about it.

Managing to avoid getting into debt in the first place is the best debt-fighting strategy available. If this is too late for you then you will need to know all about debt and how to escape it. Read on!

Not all debt is 'bad debt'

There are two main types of debt out there:

- Unsecured debt which tends to be short term in nature. This might include personal loans, credit cards and store cards.
- Secured debt which is longer term. This includes your mortgage.

When we talk about debt being a financial problem we are primarily referring to short-term unsecured debt. Not all debt is 'bad debt' from a financial planning point of view. In fact, mortgage debt is often referred to as a 'good debt' to have, particularly over the longer term. If the value of your property is rising faster than the cost of your mortgage then you are making money by having this mortgage debt in place. You only really make any money on your house if you sell it. The paper value of property might be a good talking point at dinner parties but in reality you don't really see any financial benefit from your own home unless you are in a position to sell it, repay your mortgage and you have no need to buy another place to live. This is fairly unlikely for most people during either their working or retired lives.

It is short-term unsecured debt that you need to tackle. This type of debt is rarely linked to any asset that is going to increase in value. In fact, the majority of unsecured debt is used to buy things that can only go down in value or have no resale value at all – clothes, holidays, cars, etc.

Repeat this to yourself – short-term debt is bad debt, personal loans are bad debt, credit cards are bad debt, store cards are bad debt. If you want a Money Tree with strong roots and a prospect of a healthy life you have to tackle your debt before you move on to your other financial objectives.

Your personal debt freedom day

If you live with personal debt and want to remove it from your life then you will want to have a personal debt freedom day. This is the date your can mark in your diary when your debt worries will be over. Working out your personal debt freedom day is a powerful incentive to tackle your debt and repay all of your store cards, personal loans and credit cards.

Are you ready to face your personal debt demon and beat it into submission? If so, here you go – here is my five-stage strategy for destroying your debt.

1 **Stop making it worse.** Before you start taking steps to get rid of your short-term debt you have to stop accumulating fresh debt. This will only make things worse and it will be harder to get rid of your existing problem if you are making your liabilities greater. To beat the debt you have to make it clear it isn't

welcome in your house. Remove the temptation from your life. It's a cliché, I know, but get those scissors out of your kitchen drawer and do what you must with your plastic. Sense the satisfaction as those big shears slice through the VISA, AMEX and Mastercard. You are helping yourself prevent your debt problem getting any worse.

2 **Decide first, and then get on with it.** Don't embark on a debt eradication mission until you have made the decision to win. Planning is everything but the absolute commitment to a life with no short-term debt is the winning formula. Success here comes from conviction. I'm not the world's biggest advocate of all this new age visualization stuff, but I won't deny it works. Visualize your outcome and you stand a much greater chance of reaching your goals.

3 **Know your enemy.** What are you facing? Quantify your enemy in pounds, pence and percentage points. Before you form your plan of attack you have to know what you are up against. This part of my debt-busting strategy will be painful for some. You are going to have to collate the numbers and write down your current debt position. This is the antithesis of burying your head in the sand. It's time to stare your debt straight in the eyes and work out what you have to deal with.

Take out a pad of paper and a pen, make those phone calls (or go online to check) and create the following table:

- Source of debt
- Current level of debt
- Interest rate
- Minimum monthly payment required.

4 **Make your plan of attack.** It's time to work out how you are going to tackle this debt. Take a look at the table you've just created. Find the highest interest rate and write a big number one alongside the source of this debt. Now, find the next highest rate and write a number two alongside. Work your way

through the list until each source of debt has been allocated a priority number.

You are going to start by tackling the debt with the highest rate of interest first. Fight the temptation to focus your energy (and your disposable income) on the biggest debt first. The debt that costs you the most to service each month is the debt you need to ditch most urgently. If you have a budget of £200 per month to fight £5,000 worth of debt when £600 of this debt is being charged at 17.9% and the other £4,400 is costing you 7.9%, you need to deal with the smaller debt first.

5 **Allocate your resources.** When it comes to dealing with this debt you have to work out where the resources are going to come from. It's likely that the money to clear your debt is going to come from one of two places:

■ Surplus income
■ Existing savings.

Having existing savings at the same time as short-term debt is financial madness. Use what you can to reduce the amount and then target the rest of it with your surplus income. You might need to make short-term sacrifices to reduce any unnecessary expenditure and increase this surplus income to a level that really makes a difference to the debt.

Only you can decide how important it is to eradicate your short-term debt. The priority you give this exercise will determine which sacrifices you feel able to make. If getting rid of debt is your top financial priority then it will take preference over any other desire for spending. Shopping for clothes and other luxury goods will no longer be a consideration during the time you are fighting your debt.

Some people will find this part of the plan a bit harder to manage than others. If your surplus income or existing savings are limited or non-existent then it is time to reassess your debt fighting abilities. Take a long, hard look at where your monthly income goes. This comes down to priorities again and the ability to make choices about what you need to spend and what you want to spend.

Making these choices can be really tough, especially if they involve an alteration to the way you live. Moving away from a lifestyle you have become used to over a period of years is a tough decision to make from an emotional point of view. Especially in the early days it will feel very strange and this is why it is important to continually focus on the objective and the end result.

Get support from your family and close friends. Explain to them why it is so important that you take control of your debt and also tell them when you are finding it difficult to stick to your plan. Having others around you to support you through this process will help you share the emotional burden and make the transition from debt to no debt much easier.

Being completely stuck for resources to clear your debt can sometimes lead to desperation. It is always worth remembering that there are other options available to you during this process. Your family or friends might be in a position to help you out financially for a short time. This can often be a cheaper way of borrowing money than using traditional lenders but be mindful of the potential dangers this approach can bring with it. Borrowing money from friends and family can sometimes lead to damage to existing relationships. I always suggest keeping any unofficial borrowing like this on a formal basis. If you plan to borrow from friends and family consider asking a solicitor to draw up an agreement and then stick to what you have agreed. It will keep things much happier in the long run.

However you decide to destroy your debt it is going to be hard work. Knowing this at the start might not make the fight any easier but it will mean that you go into the process with your eyes wide open. Your personal debt freedom day has to become the entire focus of your Money Tree before you can move on with the other important areas of financial planning.

Playing the credit card balance transfer game

Once you are committed to destroying your debt you need to make the job as easy as possible. One strategy for making this fight against debt go as smoothly as possible is playing the credit card balance transfer game.

If you already have money on credit cards, and you are serious about beating your debt, then you need to explore nil-rate balance transfer credit card deals. This involves getting a new credit card and asking your existing card provider to transfer the balance to this new card.

The new card offers a special interest rate for balance transfers, hopefully at 0% for a certain period of time, if you have done your homework. This means that everything you pay to your credit card company is repaying your debt and not covering the cost of interest. Doing this means that your debt is repaid faster.

As with any financial product, there are some pitfalls to watch out for:

■ The balance transfer doesn't last for ever. It might only last for six or nine months in which case you have a few options to consider. You might work out that you can afford to repay the debt by the end of the special offer period – making the end of the period the same date as your personal debt freedom day. In this case you should synchronize your payments to meet the end of the credit card term. When the special offer period runs out you will be debt free and you can cancel the card.

If you will not be able to repay the debt by the end of the offer period then you might consider becoming a 'tart'. This isn't as bad as it sounds! Being a credit card tart simply means moving your custom around between different credit card companies to take advantage of their special offers. You should be aware that being a tart has consequences. Some companies are getting wise to the activity of credit card tarts and will now impose a fee on balance transfers. There are still a few companies available that don't charge a fee – take advantage of them while you can.

If you don't fancy being a tart, having to research rates on a regular basis and move your custom around, then you might be better off looking for a 'life of balance transfer' offer. This means that the interest rate on your balance transfer stays at the same low rate for as long as it takes you to repay the debt.

- Applying for credit cards on a regular basis might damage your credit score. In fact, if you already have lots of debt and you have missed repayments or have had problems applying for credit elsewhere, you might not be able to take advantage of these special offers in the first place. To avoid hampering your credit score and putting the ability to get credit in the future in jeopardy, you should space out your credit card applications and always stick to the required repayments.

- After the balance transfer rate offer comes to an end it is likely to revert to a much higher rate. In fact, credit card companies hope that you will either forget the special offer period has come to an end or simply cannot be bothered to shop around and be a credit card tart. Charging people interest on credit card debt is how these companies make their money.

- The interest rate on balance transfers might be very low (or even zero) but it is likely to be much higher if you use the card to make new purchases. The golden rule if you play the balance transfer game is to never use the new card to buy anything. In fact, there is only one thing you should do after the card has arrived in the post and you have activated it and made the balance transfer. Take a pair of scissors and cut the card into tiny little pieces. You don't physically need the credit card to pay off your debts, only the reference numbers. Cutting up the card will stop the temptation to buy anything with it. Make sure you do the same thing with your old credit card after you make the balance transfer. You should not only cut this up but also write to the credit card company to cancel it. This stops you receiving a new card in the post a few months or a few years later when the existing card expires.

Playing the balance transfer game with credit cards can be a great way of speeding up the repayment of your debts, but it will only work well if you are disciplined. Use your diary to note the date of the end of the special balance transfer offer and also write down your repayment plans. Only use balance transfer offers from credit card companies as part of a wider strategy to pay back the money you owe.

When things get really serious

If you still have a relative level of control over your debt then my five-step strategy for destroying it will work fine. In some cases, debt gets out of control and beyond the scope of simple measures. Regardless of how much of your income you allocate to repayments, the amount is always insufficient and you have fallen into an increasing spiral of debt.

It is time to ask for help and assistance.

Once your debt gets out of control it is time to seek professional guidance. You need to eat some humble pie in two respects.

First, admit to yourself and your family that your debt has become a problem you can no longer handle on your own. This is tough for most people in this situation. They would rather bury their heads in the sand and ignore financial problems. In fact, this is the reason that bad debt problems arise in the first place.

Secondly, you have to start to communicate with the people and organizations you owe the money to, your creditors. The only way of getting out of serious debt problems is by being very honest about the problem.

If you cannot afford to pay off a particular debt then you need to negotiate with your creditors and come to an agreement about how much you can afford to pay them. If you do this by phone then it is really important to confirm what you have agreed in writing straight afterwards. Remember to only make promises to your creditors that you are in a position to keep. This is all about building trust. You started to build this trust when you picked up the phone and explained your situation. Once you have done this you need to establish the trust and then maintain it. Making a promise to pay a certain amount each month is only worth doing if you actually start making those payments.

Never pay for debt counselling advice

If you are already in a position where you have no money and spiralling debts then the last thing you should consider is paying for debt management advice. This might seem like a tempting option. Well-scripted television ads with smooth-talking presenters will offer you what seems like an easy way out of your current predicament – 'consolidate all of your debts and make one low monthly payment'.

It makes no sense to pay for advice when you don't have any money in the first place. Paying for advice will only increase your debts.

These debt management services work in quite a simple way. First, they consolidate all of your existing debts. This puts all of your debt in one place. To turn lots of little debts into one big debt they will often want to secure the debt on your home. This turns previously unsecured debts into one secured debt. If you fail to keep up repayments on a secured debt you could lose your home.

The next thing they will do is lengthen the term of your debt. They might turn short-term three- or five-year debts into fifteen- or twenty-year terms. The impact of doing this is to reduce the cost of monthly repayments.

Finally, they will add their fees for this 'service' on to your debt and probably offer you some cash (which increases your debt even further!) or offer a few months where you don't have to pay anything back (and add the repayments you are missing to your debt to make it even bigger!).

If you need help with the management of your debts then there are three places you should turn to that will not charge you a penny for their guidance and assistance. Go to these places first before you even consider paying for debt advice.

1 **The Citizens Advice Bureau (CAB).** You can find your local CAB at www.citizensadvice.org.uk.

2 **Consumer Credit Counselling Service (CCCS).** This is a debt coun- selling helpline which offers impartial advice on the best way to handle your debts. You can visit the CCCS at www.cccs.co.uk or phone them free on 0800 138 1111.

3 **National Debtline.** This is another free and impartial debt coun- selling service. As well as having a free helpline they have a number of useful publications available on their website at www.nationaldebtline.co.uk. You can call them free on 0808 808 4000.

Bankruptcy – the last resort?

Declaring bankruptcy is often seen as the last resort for dealing with serious debt problems and it has picked up a significant social stigma as a result. A lot of the rules associated with bankruptcy changed as a result of the Enterprise Act 2004. These new rules mean that you can be discharged from your bankruptcy after one year. Even with these changes it is still not an easy option or something you should treat lightly.

If you declare bankruptcy you essentially give up all of your assets to repay your debts. After about a year the rest of your debts (the ones that cannot be paid off with the value of your assets) are effectively written off. You are put back to square one (financially) and have the opportunity to make a fresh start with your financial planning.

But bankruptcy is not quite that simple.

- You have to sell your house if it contains any value over and above the level of the mortgage. If you have a partner or children who also live in the house then you might get a period of twelve months' grace while you find alternative accommodation.
- You have to close your bank account. It may be difficult to open a bank account in the future.
- You will not be allowed to act as a company director while you are an undischarged bankrupt.
- Even after the period of bankruptcy is finished you are likely to find it difficult to get any credit, and particularly difficult to get a mortgage. It is a criminal offence to try and get credit for more than £500 during the time you are bankrupt.

Before declaring bankruptcy you need to seriously consider the alternatives.

When things get serious – alternatives to bankruptcy

I hope that I've managed to convince you that bankruptcy is not an easy way to wipe the slate clean when it comes to dealing with serious debts. There are two steps that you should consider before opting for bankruptcy:

1 Individual Voluntary Arrangement (IVA)
2 Informal arrangements with creditors.

An Individual Voluntary Arrangement (IVA) is a formal agreement with your creditors that is processed through a county court. To make this happen you have to find an insolvency practitioner who will draw up an IVA proposal for your creditors; they then decide whether or not to accept it.

An IVA typically lasts between three and five years. Once the proposal has been made and agreed you have to stick to the terms or you will probably end up facing bankruptcy anyway. Remember that the services of an insolvency practitioner can be expensive and many will want you to pay their fees up front before acting on your behalf.

It is never worth paying for someone to find an insolvency practitioner on your behalf. There are firms who offer this as a service but you are always better off finding one for yourself using a phone book or the internet.

An informal arrangement is a bit like an IVA but it is not formal or legally binding. It involves you negotiating with your creditors by yourself and coming to some form of agreement with them to repay what you can of your debts. The National Debtline offers a number of free letter templates that you may want to use for inspiration when dealing with your creditors.

KEY POINTS

1 Debt is a drag on your ability to meet other financial objectives. You have to face up to and tackle debt before you can grow your Money Tree.

2 Debt is all about choice – having something now and paying for it later or saving for something now and owning it later. The choices you make and your attitude to debt will influence your ability to fight it.

3 There is a big difference between unsecured and secured debt which you need to understand and appreciate to improve your relationship with money. Unsecured short-term debt is rarely 'good debt' and this is where you should focus your debt fighting attention.

4 Follow my five-step debt destroying strategy to find your own personal debt freedom day. Make your plan and then stick to it.

5 Do everything you can to make fighting your debt easier. This includes playing the credit card balance transfer game. But watch out for the pitfalls.

6 When your debt problems become really serious it is time to ask for help. There are sources of free advice that you should turn to before paying for debt consolidation services.

7 Bankruptcy might seem like the only way out but it is not an easy option. Consider negotiating with your creditors or putting an Individual Voluntary Arrangement (IVA) in place before resorting to bankruptcy. Always seek professional advice.

Taking control of tax

> In this world nothing is certain but death and taxes.
>
> Benjamin Franklin (1706–1790)

02

Franklin may have had a point, but while paying tax is an unfortunate certainty in life, we can all do more to pay only what we have to.

Tax, in its many forms, affects us every day of our lives. I cannot imagine a day passing where we are not exposed to at least one form of tax. Just doing our jobs and earning a salary sees us paying income tax and National Insurance. Buying most things, from a house to filling up with petrol, involves paying tax.

With so many different types of tax to pay it is a wonder that we hold on to any of our money at all! This chapter is all about making sure you only pay the tax you have to and don't end up needlessly giving away your hard-earned money if you don't have to.

Avoid or evade?

When you are tax planning it is important to make the distinction between avoiding tax and evading it.

To *avoid* tax is perfectly legal. This is what tax planners, IFAs and accountants spend their days doing for their clients. Avoiding tax involves making use of available exemptions and strategies to pay less tax.

This is not something that is the preserve of the super-wealthy. Some tax avoidance can be made possible through financial common sense.

To *evade* tax is a criminal offence. Don't do it. You will be caught and the penalties can be severe. Ignorance is no defence in law. Not knowing that something is illegal will not get you out of trouble when the Revenue catch up with you and find out what you have done (or failed to do!).

There are very few 'clever' ways left of avoiding tax. If you hear about some newfangled way of paying a bit less tax, then take it with a pinch of salt. It's more than likely that it is:

a. A way of delaying the payment of tax rather than avoiding it altogether; or,

b. Poses a high level of risk to the security of your money; or,

c. Illegal.

If you are really unlucky it might even be all three.

Tax, duties and more taxes

If you spent a couple of minutes now jotting down the names of all the different types of tax, I bet your list would make it into double figures. When you consider all of the main types along with the 'stealth' taxes that we all have to pay, it can be confusing to try and understand how they all work. It becomes more difficult when you remember that a lot of taxes are not even referred to as a tax!

I'm not going to spend too much time here talking about National Insurance contributions, stamp duty, value added tax (VAT) or petrol duty. These taxes and duties have become a fact of life and there is little that we can do to avoid (not evade) them.

It is possible, however, to use simple planning techniques to avoid paying too much when it comes to the main types of tax. There are only three you have to be aware of and understand in order to improve your grasp of tax and ensure you only pay what you have to.

1 The tax you pay on your what you earn – income tax

2 The tax you pay on your investments – capital gains tax (CGT)

3 The tax your family pay when you die – inheritance tax (IHT).

This chapter takes a look at each of these types of tax in turn to explain how they work and what you can do to avoid paying too much. Whether you pay a little tax or a lot of it, there are methods for ensuring that you structure your financial plans to pay as little as possible. It's just a case of knowing how things work and then taking advantage of the reliefs and exemptions available to everyone.

Understanding income tax

Income tax is the percentage of the money you earn that you have to pay as tax. This is a system that works in tiers, as shown in the figure.

To start with, everyone has a personal allowance which is a tier you don't pay any tax at all on. This tax-free tier means that you can earn a certain amount each and every year without having to pay any income tax on it. For the 2006/07 tax year every man, woman and child in the UK gets a personal allowance of £5,035.

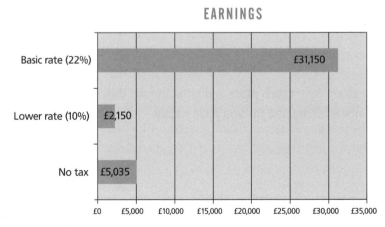

Income tax brackets

In fact, once you reach age 65 your personal allowance gets bigger (£7,280) and then it is increased again at age 75 to £7,420.

The next tier is the 10% band. This is a much smaller tier and you have to pay income tax at the rate of 10% on this amount of income. We call this the lower rate tax band: it applies to the first £2,150 of your income for the 2006/07 tax year.

The tier after this is the 22% or basic rate tax band. The majority of most people's income falls into this band. Because income tax works on a tiered system this doesn't mean that basic rate taxpayers pay 22% income tax on all of their income. It's only the income you earn that falls within this tier that gets taxed at the basic rate. Some of your income is still free of tax and some only taxed at 10%. During 2006/07 the basic rate tax band is applied from £2,151 to £33,300 of your earnings, after the personal allowance has been taken into account.

The top tier of income tax is the higher rate tax band. This is the money you pay 40% income tax on. Again, a higher rate taxpayer doesn't pay 40% income tax on all of their earnings. They have some tax-free earnings, some lower rate and some basic rate as well. Higher rate income tax is paid on earnings over £33,300 for the 2006/07 tax year.

Remember that every tax year your personal allowance and the income tax bands will change. They typically increase but it is worth keeping an eye on the Budget each year to find out what changes have taken place and what impact this will have on the amount of income tax you have to pay.

Some popular income tax misconceptions

While income tax is simple, people often have some very strange ideas about how the system works. It's time to shatter some popular income tax misconceptions.

- **Offshore earnings are tax free.** Not true. As a UK taxpayer you are subject to UK income tax on your worldwide earnings. There are certain offshore investment schemes that enable you to delay the payment of income tax, but there is no such thing as tax-free income for a UK taxpayer.

- **There is a student or child's rate of income tax.** Not true. Everyone is subject to the same income tax system, regardless of their age or occupation. Students pay income tax in the same way that full-time employees do. So do babies and children (if they have sufficient income to warrant paying tax).

- **It's not worth earning more money because you have to pay more tax.** Not true. This is still a popular income tax misconception because people don't always understand the tiered system of income tax. While getting a pay rise can sometimes push people into a higher rate tax band, this doesn't have an effect on your total earnings. Only your earnings in the higher rate band get taxed at the higher rate of income tax. A pay rise will not suddenly mean that all of your income is taxed at 40%.

- **Income tax is charged at the same rate for all types of earnings.** Not true. There are actually different rates of income tax depending on the source of the money. For earned income (your salary from employment for example) the rates are 10%, 22% and 40%. Savings income (for example, interest on your building society account) gets charged at 10%, 20% and 40%. The other type of income is dividend income that you might get if you are a shareholder of a limited company or have stock market investments. The rate of tax on this is 10% for income up to the basic rate and 32.5% for the higher rate.

How to pay less income tax

Paying less income tax isn't about using the most exotic high-risk tax saving scheme you can find. There are a few of these incredibly creative schemes around at any one time. They often cost a lot of money to use, involve a higher than average risk to the capital value of your money and can raise some serious questions from the tax inspector. These are all things you should strive to avoid, particularly an investigation from HM Revenue & Customs.

Smart investors ensure that their Money Tree pays the correct amount of tax and pays it promptly. Tax is one area of your financial life that can draw unwelcome attention from HMRC and create unnecessary hassle. It is always best to pay what you owe and pay it on time.

That being said, you should always ensure that you are using all of the basic steps available to you to pay less income tax. Each year people waste hundreds of pounds on income tax because they fail to use some simple steps.

At this stage I will let you in on a little secret. It is much easier to save money on your income tax bill if you are either a married couple or a higher rate taxpayer. Single and/or basic rate taxpayers are rather limited when it comes to techniques for saving on income tax, but there is something for everyone!

1 View your tax planning as a couple if you are married

Let's assume that one spouse is earning a salary and the other is not. All of a sudden you have the personal allowance of the non-earning spouse to play with. The most effective way of using this allowance is normally to register any savings in the name of the non-earning spouse. This way any interest generated from the savings can be paid gross (tax-free) and there is no basic rate or higher rate income tax liability on the money. Non-earners can elect to receive their interest gross by completing form R85. Just ask at your bank or building society and they should be able to point you in the right direction. For the 2006/07 tax year a non-earning spouse could earn up to £5,035 of interest without having to pay a penny in income tax. It would take over £100,000 in savings earning gross interest of 5% per annum to generate this much interest.

2 Make pension contributions

The greatest thing about making pension contributions is the immediate income tax relief you are awarded. This is applied in two parts. You don't get to really feel the benefit of the basic rate income tax relief; it is simply added directly to the pension fund to boost the value of your contribution. The really fun part comes along if you are a higher rate taxpayer. As a higher rate taxpayer you get the value of the pension contribution, after the addition of basic rate income tax, added to your basic rate income tax band. This means that more of your earnings will fall into the basic rate tax band and less will be subject to higher rate income tax. The effective tax saving on this is 18% (the difference between the basic and higher rate tax rates). It means that a higher rate taxpayer paying a net pension contribution of £250 per month will save almost £700 a year in higher rate income tax.

3 Use your cash ISA allowance each tax year

You can protect up to £3,000 of your savings from the ravages of income tax each year. All you have to do is make use of your Mini Cash Individual Savings Account (ISA) allowance. Each and every person in the UK over the age of 16 is allowed to have one Mini Cash ISA each year, as long as you haven't already opened a Maxi ISA. Moving your money from savings to a cash ISA makes perfect sense because interest within the ISA is not subject to any income tax. In fact, it is paid gross while your bank or building society interest is paid out net of income tax. The impact of this on £3,000 may not be massive. Assuming a 5% gross interest rate it would mean a saving of £30 a year for a basic rate taxpayer and £60 a year for a higher rate taxpayer. But let's assume that you use your ISA allowance every year for five tax years. All of a sudden we are talking about £15,000 of cash sheltered from the tax inspector. If your spouse does the same then £30,000 could be free of income tax within the same period of time. The income tax saving on £30,000 is £300 a year for a basic rate taxpayer and £600 for a higher rate taxpayer. Not something to be sniffed at!

Don't break the rules when it comes to ISAs. As I explain on p. 131, you cannot have a Maxi and a Mini ISA in the same tax year.

4 Make sure you have the right tax code

If you are employed then your income tax is automatically taken through a system known as Pay As You Earn (or PAYE). The amount of income tax you pay through PAYE will depend upon your tax code. If you have recently moved jobs or you think that you are paying over the odds in terms of income tax then it may be worth writing to your local tax office and asking them to check your tax code.

5 Invest in a Venture Capital Trust (VCT)

If you have an appetite for a high level of risk then an investment in a VCT is a great way of reducing your income tax bill. You can invest up to £200,000 each year in a VCT and new investments get 30% income tax relief. The only caveat is that you have to hold on to the investment for a minimum period of at least five years. VCT investment is not for the faint-hearted as it involves investing your money in smaller unproven companies that could go bust as easily as they could succeed. It is a high-risk game but the income tax relief makes it attractive for many income tax payers.

Understanding capital gains tax

When you make an investment and it goes up in value, you have to pay tax on the gain when you sell the investment. This is known as capital gains tax (CGT) and it can really eat away at those profits you were so proud of achieving.

To start with, there are a number of assets that are not subject to CGT when you sell them. These include:

- Your home (as long as it was your only home during the time your owned it)
- Your car (as long as it is a private vehicle)
- Cash held in sterling currency
- Moveable objects that are valued at £6,000 or less.

So, for example, if you bought some shares for £10,000 and they were worth £35,000 when you decided to sell them ten years later, you could be faced with a tax charge on the £25,000 investment gain. However, if you bought a house for £185,000 and sold it for £215,000 after four years there would be no capital gains tax to pay, assuming it was your main residence.

CGT is calculated by adding the investment gain on to your income to establish which rate it will be taxed at. For example, if you are already a higher rate taxpayer then your capital gains will be taxed at the higher rate, 40%. As a non-taxpayer your capital gains will work their way through the normal income tax bands, starting with the nil income tax environment of the personal allowance.

There are some ways of reducing the amount of CGT you have to pay. If you don't invest your money or sell any of your assets then you may never have to pay CGT, but as someone keen to grow their Money Tree it is more likely that you will fall into the realm of the CGT monster before too long. It pays to be prepared before your first encounter with this particular beast!

To avoid CGT you have to understand some of the rules. It is one of the more complex areas of tax planning and it can be a wise investment to engage an accountant if you have a particularly complicated set of capital gains to calculate.

CGT is applied to more or less any other asset you might own and sell for more than you paid for it. It is possible to reduce the amount you pay by identifying as many available exemptions, reliefs and allowances as possible. Here are some of the main things you should keep an eye out for if you have a potential CGT charge to pay.

Top Tips for capital gains tax

■ Every year you get an annual exemption. This is an amount of capital gain that isn't subject to tax. It means that you can dispose of assets each year, up to a certain value, without having to worry about CGT. In fact, this annual exemption is the reason why most people will never have to worry about paying CGT. For the 2006/07 tax year it has been set at £8,800.

■ Moving assets between a husband and wife (who are living together) does not create a CGT issue. Giving your spouse ownership of an investment or other asset on which you have made a capital gain is not treated as a 'disposal' for CGT purposes.

■ If you have held your assets for a long time then not all of the gain is subject to CGT. Since April 1998 a system called Taper Relief has been in place that reduces the amount of capital gain that you are taxed on. In fact, the longer you own the assets, the less of the gain you have to pay tax on. Once you have owned an asset for three years the amount of the gain starts to be reduced. You have to hold on to the asset for at least ten years to get the maximum amount of Taper Relief available, where only 60% of the gain is chargeable.

■ If you have owned the asset for a really long time then something called Indexation Allowance can reduce the amount of the gain even further. This only applies to assets owned before April 1998 and was replaced by the introduction of Taper Relief in that year. If you have owned an asset for this long and think you might be entitled to Indexation Allowance then I strongly advise you to seek professional advice from an accountant.

■ The cost of buying or acquiring and selling or disposing of the asset can be knocked off the gain before you calculate how much tax you owe. These incidental expenses might include the fees you had to pay when you purchased the asset and also costs like stamp duty.

■ You can also knock off any costs involved in the enhancement of the asset. Unfortunately normal maintenance or repair costs are not included in this category.

Understanding inheritance tax

Inheritance tax used to be a problem that would only affect the super-wealthy, but no longer. The recent rapid rise in UK house prices has meant that more and more households have fallen into the price bracket that could become subject to IHT if a death took place.

Let's start with some basics. IHT is a form of tax paid on the value of your estate when you die. This means that you don't actually have to pay the IHT, but the people you leave your property to will.

IHT is a fairly punishing form of tax. It is charged at the rate of 40%. Every person has a nil-rate band when it comes to IHT; for 2006/07 this is set at £285,000. This means that the first £285,000 of your estate is charged at 0% but anything above this level is charged at 40%.

But inheritance tax is often called a 'voluntary tax'. Most competent financial planners should be able to help you construct a strategy for reducing or removing a potential IHT liability with sensible use of your will and some trusts. The problem with this is that reducing IHT is a balancing act between effectiveness and control. If you want your IHT reduction plans to be really effective then you have to give up a lot of control over your cash. The most effective plans involve giving up the greatest level of control over your money.

I find that clients fall into one of two categories when it comes to IHT planning. They either want to do everything possible to avoid paying even a penny of inheritance tax to the Treasury or they are happy that their children will receive more of an inheritance (even after paying tax) than they ever did. When it comes to estate planning opinion tends to be polarized, and both views are equally valid. There is nothing wrong with not wanting to plan to avoid inheritance tax. The rise in the general level of wealth in this country means that future generations will indeed benefit from much higher levels of inheritance than their parents or grandparents ever did. On the other hand, where some simple tax planning tools are available it makes perfect sense to take advantage of them.

Some ways to pay less inheritance tax

There are plenty of exotic schemes to reduce the amount of inheritance tax your beneficiaries will eventually have to pay on your estate. In the 2006 Budget the Chancellor took the unprecedented step of introducing new rules that would make a lot of these schemes less attractive. By introducing an initial and periodic tax charge to certain types of trusts, he ensured that only the simple steps of reducing an inheritance tax liability would remain attractive to the wider population.

Because of the added complexities now involved with inheritance tax planning, it pays to seek proper advice. The best professional adviser to speak to on this subject is either an independent financial adviser who holds the Advanced Financial Planning Certificate (AFPC) qualification G10: Taxation and Trusts, or a solicitor who is a member of the Society of Trust and Estate Practitioners (STEP).

Planning to reduce inheritance tax can be a very emotive subject. You must remember at all times that you are discussing a tax charge that is going to occur when somebody dies. Making important decisions about inheritance tax will often involve input from many members of the family. If you sense that somebody is getting upset during this particular discussion then it is worth coming back to the subject on another occasion. Always use your discretion to decide on the most appropriate time to raise inheritance tax and estate planning. For some it can be a touchy area but for others open discussion brings a sense of relief that plans have been put in place for the future.

1 Make a proper will

We have this message drummed into us from an early age yet I still find that people come to see me and they haven't written a will. Even worse, they have a will in place but it is out of date and no longer reflects their wishes. Most wills that are in place and up to date make a provision to leave everything to the surviving spouse. While this is very noble it is important to remember that there is no inheritance tax to pay on transfers of assets between spouses anyway. By doing this you are effectively wasting the nil-rate band of the spouse who dies. On the death of the second spouse only one nil-rate band is available and this increases the potential inheritance tax bill for your children and other beneficiaries. It makes more sense to use a trust within your will to preserve the nil-rate band of the first spouse to die so on the second death you make effective use of a double nil-rate band – worth £570,000 in the 2006/07 tax year.

Giving away control of your money by setting up a trust when the first spouse dies is something to be treated with caution as the surviving spouse will want the knowledge that they have sufficient financial resources available to them. This form of will trust planning is very popular for the simple reason that the surviving spouse keeps their financial security but in the longer term the inheritance tax reduction still takes place.

2 Take advantage of the seven year trick

If you give an asset to your beneficiaries and then die after seven years there is no inheritance tax to pay. This type of gift is known as a 'potentially exempt transfer' or PET. The amount of the gift that is liable to inheritance tax reduces over the seven-year period on a sliding scale. If you survive for over three years your liability reduces to 80% and this falls away to 20% after six years. Because it is difficult to guarantee that you will survive for at least seven years after making such a gift it makes sense to insure against the risk of dying early and creating an inheritance tax problem. This is possible using term assurance (because you need cover for a set period of time) that has a decreasing sum assured (because the potential IHT liability is reducing over time).

3 Give your money away!

You are able to make certain gifts within your lifetime that become immediately exempt from inheritance tax. The rules allow every person to make a gift of £3,000 in each tax year. If you don't make use of your annual exemption in one tax year then all is not lost. It is possible to carry it forward to the next tax year and make an exempt gift of up to £6,000 instead.

It is also possible to make small gifts of up to £250 to any person. If your child is getting married then there is a gift exemption of £5,000. Grandparents can give their grandchildren a wedding gift of up to £2,500 without having to worry about inheritance tax and any other person can make a wedding gift of up to £1,000 within these gift limits. These gifts immediately drop out of the value of your estate for the purposes of calculating inheritance tax. The argument for making gifts is strong if you will not miss the money and plan to give it away after your death anyway. At least by making gifts during your lifetime you get to see the recipient enjoy the gift!

4 Make gifts as part of your normal expenditure

Another way of reducing the value of your estate (and hence leaving less to be assessed for inheritance tax purposes) is to give away money out of your income. The way to claim this exemption is to prove that the gifts are made out of after-tax income (rather than your savings) and also that they are made on a regular basis. This means that a gift you make every month is likely to be seen as having been made out of normal expenditure. You can use this exemption to fund the cost of a life assurance policy that will eventually pay for the costs of your inheritance tax liability. More on this in the next tip!

5 Insure against the IHT bill

In Tip Number Two I have already talked about how to insure against dying within the seven year period of a potentially exempt transfer by using decreasing term assurance. There is another type of life assurance that is often used to cover the entire cost of an inheritance tax bill. This is called whole of life assurance. The way this type of life assurance typically works when it comes to inheritance tax planning is to provide a sum assured equivalent to the potential amount of IHT to be paid. In the case of a married couple the policy would be established on a joint life second death basis so the sum assured would not become payable until the death of the second spouse (the time when the money is needed to pay the IHT bill). It is best to set this up on a whole of life rather than a term assurance basis simply because you don't know how long you will need to have the cover in place. While the cost of this life cover can be met from normal expenditure by the people actually covered I often encourage my clients to ask their children to meet the costs of the life assurance. It is the children who will see the benefit from having the cover in place as it will reduce the IHT bill and increase their inheritance. If the children refuse to pay the whole amount then at least get them to contribute towards part of the cost.

A gentle approach is always best here but as with any financial discussion make sure that you are very clear about the objectives. I'm an advocate of making informal financial arrangements more formal wherever possible. There is no harm in making sure that everyone knows exactly where they stand when it comes to this type of financial planning.

KEY POINTS

1 Tax is a root of the Money Tree. Getting to grips with the three main types of tax – income tax, capital gains tax and inheritance tax – will give your Money Tree some strong roots.

2 It is perfectly legal (and advisable) to avoid tax but illegal and dangerous to evade it. Simple steps are better than sophisticated and complex tax avoidance schemes.

3 Income tax is a tiered system. It is easier to avoid if you are married and/or a higher rate taxpayer. By making use of available income tax relief from various investment schemes you can easily save hundreds of pounds in income tax each year.

4 Capital gains tax eats away at your investment gains but there are plenty of ways to reduce what you have to pay. Understand the exemptions and pay less tax. The services of an accountant can be a wise investment if you have complex affairs when it comes to capital gains.

5 Inheritance tax is a voluntary tax, but reducing it means giving up control or ownership of your cash. If you are a married couple or in a civil partnership don't waste the nil-rate band of the first partner to die. Some basic planning with your will is essential to save many thousands of pounds in inheritance tax.

Serious about savings

> Saving is a fine thing. Especially when your parents have done it for you.
>
> Winston Churchill (1874–1965)

03

All about cash

Cash is the foundation of any financial plan. Some people say that 'cash is king'. I know many savvy investors who see it as the cornerstone of their entire investment portfolio.

We don't seem to have much in the way of a 'savings culture' in this country these days. People prefer a 'spend today, suffer later' philosophy that has led to rising levels of personal debt.

Having a positive savings attitude will ensure that your Money Tree has solid roots. In fact, trying to move on to longer term and more complex financial objectives without getting this right will lead to disappointment and potential disaster for your finances.

Getting savings right really comes down to attitude. Some people have the 'right' attitude when it comes to saving money and some don't. People will argue that you are born a saver. I would argue that anyone can become a saver, even if they didn't pick up the saving ethic from their family.

I know people who developed their own very positive attitude to savings as they grew up. They made saving their money second nature: it became a habit for these people. They didn't think about this course of action, it simply happened because it was something they did regularly when young. By making regular saving a habit rather than a chore you can substantially improve your chances of financial success.

Whenever you buy something you are faced with two main choices:

- You can either save for the item and buy it with your own money (save now, buy it later), or
- You can buy the item with other people's money and then pay them back (buy it now, pay later).

Take a moment to think about an expensive item that you really want. Which of the two options above appeals to you the most? Are you the sort of person that reaches for the credit card or are you a savvy saver who prefers to feel the satisfaction of saving for the item and buying it when you can actually afford it?

Top Tips to get a better rate of interest

When it comes to saving your money you will want to ensure that you are getting the best rate of interest available. Getting more interest on your savings takes a small amount of work, but it is something you should be able to do in a couple of hours. The benefit could be tens or even hundreds of pounds of extra cash each year. The more you have in savings, the more it is worth the little bit of effort involved.

1 Use a Mini Cash ISA

Getting your savings into a tax-free environment means less of your interest goes to the tax department and more goes into your pocket. Anyone who is 16 or older can put up to £3,000 into a Mini Cash ISA each and every tax year. If you are married then don't forget to make use of your spouse's Mini Cash ISA allowance as well as your own to effectively double your maximum to £6,000. As well as getting tax-free interest you will also discover that the best interest rates are reserved for Mini Cash ISA accounts. Still, make sure that you always shop around and do your homework before putting your money into an ISA. The difference between the best and worst interest rates can be massive and your own bank or building society is not necessarily the best place to go for a competitive rate.

Bear in mind that if you open a Mini Cash ISA then you cannot open a Maxi ISA during the same tax year. You can still invest up to £4,000 in a Stocks & Shares Mini ISA, so the two maximum limits add up to the same £7,000 available from a Maxi ISA, but from different components.

2 Lump your cash together

By putting more of your money into a savings account you can normally qualify for a better rate of interest. Banks and building societies sometimes reserve their top rates of interest on savings accounts for people who save more money. Keeping your savings in a number of different savings accounts will therefore reduce your potential for getting the best rates.

3 Give some notice

A notice savings account means that you have to tell your bank or building society in advance if you plan to withdraw any money. These notice accounts tend to offer a higher rate of interest than instant access accounts. The only downside to this type of account is that you lose the ability to get hold of your money before the end of the selected notice period. If you do take money out of the account sooner than this you will be penalized with lost interest (earned before the withdrawal took place). If you are able to, give notice before getting hold of your cash then choose the longest notice period possible to get the best rate of interest. Typical notice periods are 30, 60 and 90 days, so make sure you choose a notice period that works best for you.

4 Shop around

Never rest on your laurels. Once you have found a competitive interest rate it is important to ensure it stays competitive. Make sure that you review your interest rates at least once a year. In fact, once you have found a great rate put a note in your diary for a year's time and commit yourself to shopping around again when this date comes around.

5 Watch out for introductory rates

A trick that the banks and building societies love to play is offering a high headline interest rate that includes a special offer for a limited period of time. This means that your interest rate might seem pretty good for a while, but it will suddenly look much worse after that. This is another reason to always read the small print when choosing a savings account (or any type of financial product). Take advantage of introductory offers or bonuses if you are prepared to make the effort to shop around again when they come to an end, but avoid them at all costs if you are looking for a longer-term home for your savings.

Why save?

Saving money is an alien concept to many. When there is the temptation to have something today by putting it on plastic your heart can often rule your head. This has created a massive increase in the level of personal debt over the last ten years. Being able to separate the emotional reasons for buying from practical ones is an important discipline when it comes to saving.

There are two main reasons that you might want to save your money:

- For a specific short-term purpose or financial goal, such as buying a sofa or saving the deposit to enable you to buy a property
- To create an emergency fund to soften the financial blow of any unexpected events or changes to your circumstances.

Saving for a purpose

One reason for saving is that it is cheaper than buying goods or services on a credit or store card. Buying something with a credit card means you have to pay interest charges for the privilege. It costs you money. Saving your money and waiting to buy that same item with your own cash means you don't incur these interest charges. In fact, you are rewarded for saving by the addition of interest.

Cash is what we call a 'liquid' asset. This means that it is easy to get your hands on in an emergency. A liquid asset doesn't take much time to get hold of. A good example of an illiquid asset is your house. It might have a value, but getting your hands on that value can be difficult and time-consuming.

Because you don't have to find a buyer before you can get your cash, it is easily accessible. This is why it is such an attractive asset class to use when you have either a specific short-term goal in mind or might need the money in an emergency.

Building an emergency fund

When I carry out financial planning or investment work with clients I always encourage them to hold some money back. Even if they are investing many hundreds of thousands of pounds in the different investment asset classes I always recommend that some stays in cash.

Your emergency fund is your 'rainy day' money. Chapter 05 examines the various protection plans you might put in place to ensure you are not too financially disadvantaged if things go wrong. There is a step to consider before buying protection and that involves saving up a sum of money that you can easily access if you need it.

There are no hard and fast rules about the right amount of money to keep in an emergency fund. A typical suggestion is to have a savings fund that contains three months' pay. This is net pay (what you would actually get in your pocket for three months' work). The rationale behind this suggestion is that you should be able to find work within a three-month period. The 'right' amount of money to keep in your emergency fund will very much depend on your circumstances. You might be in a position where you have an easy means of getting money from a relative, friend or your business that means an emergency fund is less important to you.

Do make sure that your emergency fund is relatively easy to get hold of. As the name suggests, this is money you will need in case of emergency so don't tie it up for months on end in a 90-day notice account. It is also important that the value of your emergency fund stays relatively stable. Cash is a good choice because you can be sure that the value will not go down from month to month. When you need to get access to your fund you will know exactly how much is there for you.

You may choose to put your emergency fund into a short-term notice account (30 days for example). This gives you a good mix between getting easy access to your money and getting a good rate of interest. It will also discourage you from using the money in anything other than a real emergency.

Only you can decide what constitutes a real emergency and a genuine reason to use this fund. It might be worth making a list of genuine emergencies that you keep in a safe place. If your perceived emergency doesn't match one of the items on the list then don't allow yourself to use the money.

Getting to the position where you have three months' pay in a savings account might not happen for you overnight. It will certainly take you longer than three months, because everyone has expenses to meet from their monthly income. Don't worry if it takes you two years or more to build your emergency fund. Just remember how long it took you to create the fund when you are tempted to spend the money on anything other than a real crisis.

Cash as an asset class

In Chapter 06 I will introduce you to an investment concept called 'asset allocation'. When we talk about investing money and allocating it between different asset classes, we have to consider four main types.

The first main asset class is 'cash'. Cash as an asset class has some unique characteristics that make it very different from the other types of investments available to you:

■ The capital value doesn't go down. Unlike investments in property or equities, the value of your cash is not in danger of going down.

■ The 'real' value of cash is eroded over time by the effects of inflation. Inflation means that things cost more as time goes on. Because cash doesn't grow very quickly in value it has a very limited ability to keep pace with the rate of inflation. Over time the value of your cash will be less than it is today because things will become more expensive.

■ Cash doesn't fall in value but it doesn't grow in value either. The addition of interest is, in fact, income rather than capital growth. Most bank or building society savings accounts are set up to simply add this interest income to the value of the cash rather than distribute it to you.

Where can you save your money?

The most common place to save your cash is in a bank or building society savings account. You keep your money in the savings account and, in return, the bank or building society adds some interest on a monthly or yearly basis as a reward.

In fact, the bank or building society is making use of your cash to be able to reward you with the interest. They typically lend your money (or at least a pooled collection of all the money in savings) for which they are paid. They lend the money at a higher cost than the interest they pay you for saving with them, and this is how they make their profits.

An alternative to saving with a bank or building society is to consider the range of savings vehicles on offer from National Savings & Investments. This is backed by HM Treasury which makes it a very secure home for your money.

The most interesting product on offer from National Savings & Investments is probably Premium Bonds. These are actually an investment rather than a cash product, but they share similar attributes to cash that make them worthy of a mention here. You can invest from a minimum of £100 up to a maximum of £30,000 for any length of time you like. Instead of receiving interest on your money you are entered into a prize draw each month and stand the chance of winning a tax-free prize. These prizes range from £50 to £1m (two of the £1m jackpots are paid out each month).

Because you don't get any interest on the money held in Premium Bonds their real value can go down over time as a result of the effects of inflation. However, if you hold on to them for long enough you would hope that any prizes you win would at least make up for this lost interest!

Premium Bonds have been around for over fifty years now and their popularity among savers does not appear to be fading. They are a bit more interesting than keeping your money in the building society but just as safe and almost as accessible.

While you don't get any interest on the money held within Premium Bonds they do use a nominal rate of interest to calculate the total prize fund each month. At the time of writing this was 3% – not bad when you consider that prizes are paid free of tax.

What about the downside?

While cash forms an important part of your Money Tree, it is important to remember that it has some limitations as well as benefits. The biggest drawback to keeping your money in cash is the effect of inflation. This means that goods and services become more expensive, they go up in price. Inflation is a measure of how much the price of goods and services rise over time.

The drawback of cash therefore is that it doesn't tend to keep pace with the rate of inflation. This means that the longer you hold on to cash, the less it will be worth in real terms. You will be able to buy less with the same amount of cash in ten years' time as you could today. Even with the addition of interest it is unlikely that cash will be able to keep pace with inflation.

It is therefore important not to hold on to your cash for too long. I would suggest that the maximum length of time you keep money in cash is around five years. If your purpose for saving is likely to take longer than five years then you should consider investment rather than savings. The distinction between savings and investment is really down to:

- The length of time you want to keep the money for before using it
- How much risk you feel comfortable taking with your money
- How much capital growth or income you want to get from your money.

Some people will feel more comfortable sticking to savings rather than investment for a longer period of time. There is nothing wrong with this, particularly if you are a very cautious person when it comes to investment risk. But you should be aware what the downside of this approach is and also that you might get better returns by investing your money.

Other people hold on to cash simply because they don't know for sure what the timescale they are saving for is. This is often the case when saving for a deposit on a house. You might have a target date in mind for buying but you never know when the right property will come on to the market, at which time you might need to get your hands on the money in a hurry. Having to risk that the value of your funds have dropped a bit at that time because it is subject to investment risk might not be acceptable.

The other potential downside of cash is the risk that the place you save your money could collapse. I'm not talking about a building falling down here, but rather the financial collapse of a bank or building society. Under normal circumstances you would expect that your capital in such an account would be completely secure. If you saved £100 then you would have a reasonable expectation of getting at least £100 back (plus the addition of some interest).

Building societies are protected by the Financial Services Compensation Scheme (FSCS). Having to fall back on this would be the last resort but it would give you some financial security if your bank or building society were to get into serious financial trouble. The FSCS does come with some limitations that you should know about. It will only pay out up to a maximum of £31,700 per person based on the money you have in savings. Of this maximum limit, 100% cover is provided on the first £2,000 and then 90% is paid on the next £33,000. This means that if you have more than £35,000 in savings the FSCS will not pay compensation based on the full amount.

But even with this compensation scheme in place, just how safe is your money in the bank or building society? Within the banking sector there is certainly some history of significant financial collapse of high profile banks. What is more likely to happen with a building society in financial trouble is that one of its competitors would buy it out to protect the overall reputation of the building society sector. Saving your money in a bank or building society is not completely without risk, but with the checks and measures in place, along with the added protection of the Financial Services Compensation Scheme, you can save your money in these institutions with relative peace of mind.

High headline interest rates on regular saver accounts

I've noticed recently that a number of banks have been trying to tempt customers to save with them regularly by offering very high headline rates of interest. In a lot of cases these rates of interest have been more than twice that on offer for ordinary savings accounts. These regular savings accounts come with a lot of small print, so here are some of the main points to be aware of and watch out for:

■ You don't really get the headline interest rate. Eight or ten per cent interest might look very attractive but in reality you will be getting much less than this on your savings. Here's why. In month one you will get the full amount of interest on that month's savings over the next twelve months. However, in month two your savings will only be invested for eleven months, so you only get $^{11}/_{12}$ of the headline interest rate. In fact, as each month goes on your money saved that month is invested for less time.

■ At the end of the twelve months the interest rate plummets. Very often the headline interest rate on offer is only for a limited period. After this promotional period (typically twelve months) the interest rate drops right down to the normal low rate of interest on a typical savings account. Banks rely on inertia; most savers will not bother to move their savings at this point. Instead they hope that you will leave your money where it is, earning a pitifully low rate of interest. Remember to review your savings after twelve months and see if you could do better somewhere else!

- You have to pay your salary into their account as well. One of the biggest catches that comes with these high headline interest rate regular savings accounts is having to make regular payments into a current account with the same bank. You should make your banking decisions based on value and service rather than a tempting interest rate on your regular savings.

- Your maximum savings each month are limited. Even if you do decide that the interest rate on offer is extremely competitive, you will be severely restricted when it comes to putting money into the account. Most place a cap of £250 a month on your regular savings so if you want to get the high interest rate you are limited in how much money you can save.

The lesson to be learnt here is 'always read the small print'. The big banks and building societies have large marketing departments that think up interesting and exciting ways to get your custom and entice you to part with your hard-earned cash. It is your job to look beyond that marketing 'spin' and find the real deals on the high street. Ignore headline rates on big posters and dig a bit deeper before making decisions about your savings. There are some good deals out there, but they rarely shout about themselves.

Encouraging the savings habit

The recent launch of the Child Trust Fund in 2005 has brought the subject of saving for the future of your children into the limelight. If you have children then you will already know about the day-to-day costs you have to cover. What you might not have paid much attention to (yet!) are the potential outgoings you might want to meet. With the cost of tertiary education, a first car, a wedding for one or more children, the deposit on a property and business start-up costs, there is certainly a lot to budget and plan for.

The thought of paying for all or any of these future expenses from income is unrealistic. Most of them are capital costs that require long-term saving or investment to put yourself in a position where you can comfortably afford them.

Not everyone will be so enthusiastic about meeting these future costs for their children. I know that a lot of parents will do everything in their power to give their offspring a financially stable start in adult life. Without careful saving and planning it would be completely unaffordable to try and offer any support for these events.

But saving for children is not all about building up a big enough pot of cash to pay for these things in 18 to 21 years' time. It should also include teaching your children to develop the habit of saving. The earlier you get them started with this process the better. If you can help your children develop a saving habit early in life you will be helping them to avoid financial trouble when they become adults.

My earliest memory of saving was opening a bank account that provided a savings chart to colour in and map the progress of my account. It was a simple way to encourage saving and discourage spending. Because I would colour in a section of the chart each time I paid some money into the account I was desperate to save. Receiving my pocket money and depositing it at the bank became the highlight of the week because it meant being able to colour in another level of my savings chart. I never wanted to take any money out of the account (even when I really wanted to buy a new toy or stickers for my album!) because I had already charted my progress. It was an incredibly simple but effective way to encourage children to save.

Most banks and building societies now offer savings accounts for children. In fact, there is a massive amount of choice, but it is important to look beyond the branding or free gifts which often use children's media characters to appeal to their target market. Accounts for children range from excellent to very poor. Use your judgement and comparison skills to shop around and look beyond the teddy bears and birthday cards they have on offer.

Interest on savings accounts for children is still taxed in the same way it would be for an adult, but in most cases the child will not have enough income to warrant paying income tax. This means that their savings interest will fall into the nil-rate band. Don't think for a minute that this means you can transfer savings into the name of your child to avoid tax. If you do this and more than £100 a year worth of interest is generated it gets taxed as if it belongs to you. The tax department is wise to this particular tax avoidance scheme.

KEY POINTS

1 **Cash gives your Money Tree solid roots.** Don't attempt to move on to more complex areas of your financial life until you have established a good understanding of savings. Every purchasing decision comes down to a decision between saving for the object and buying it on credit. Decide which approach you prefer and think about the longer-term financial implications.

2 **Successful saving is all about the interest.** Use the Top Tips earlier in this chapter to ensure that you are always being paid the most competitive rate. Income tax will eat away at your

savings so shelter them from tax using a Cash Mini ISA when you can. Even when you have found the most competitive rate you need to keep this under review. Once a year is an appropriate length of time to find out if you are still on the receiving end of a market-leading interest rate.

3 We save for a specific short-term purpose and to build an emergency fund that will support us when times get tough. Building your emergency fund might take some time but it is an important part of your Money Tree and should only be accessed in a real crisis. Decide what a real emergency looks like before it arises so you can decide whether or not to use your special fund.

4 There are plenty of places to save your cash. Premium Bonds from National Savings & Investments are a more interesting alternative to cash that gives you the chance of winning tax-free prizes each month. You don't get any interest on your holdings in Premium Bonds so watch out for the longer-term impact of inflation.

5 Cash might be more stable than other forms of investment but it doesn't come without some risks. The impact of inflation can erode the purchasing power of your cash over time. If you are planning to keep the money for more than five years then you might want to consider investment rather than saving. The Financial Services Compensation Scheme provides a bit of a safety net if your bank or building society gets into financial trouble, but it has limitations.

6 Regular savings accounts offer high headline rates of interest but watch out for the small print. The impact of income tax on the interest, reducing lengths of time on which your cash receives the interest and much lower interest rates at the end of the term can make an attractive headline rate look much less appealing.

7 The earlier you can start to encourage the savings habit with your children, the better. There is a wide range of savings accounts for children but you have to look beyond the free gifts and branding to make sure you get a good deal.

Making the most of your mortgage —

> Property is the fruit of labor; property is desirable; it is a positive good in the world.
>
> Abraham Lincoln (1809–1865)

04

Apart from being the single largest debt you will ever have in your life, a mortgage is your gateway to home ownership. The substantial increase in house prices over the past decade has made a large mortgage a necessary evil in the UK. Even if you have resigned yourself to a big mortgage there are important considerations in finding the right arrangement for you. Just how can you make sure that your mortgage represents a healthy branch of your Money Tree?

It's just a (really) big loan

You have to keep in mind that your mortgage is just a loan. Yes, it's a big loan. And yes, it lasts quite a bit longer than most loans normally would. At the end of the day it's just a big loan. But a mortgage is a big loan with a function.

Having a mortgage enables you to buy a house (or flat, apartment, or castle). This means that your really big loan serves a purpose. It becomes your ticket to home ownership and an investment in the property asset class. A lot of people forget this and just see their mortgage as a burden throughout their lives.

This chapter begins with the mortgage basics. I start by explaining the different types of mortgage you might be faced with. Like all financial products, mortgages come in a variety of flavours. Some of these flavours are better than others but all have their own peculiar quirks. By understanding the basics you will be able to go shopping for a mortgage fully armed with what you need to know.

I then look at how to choose the right sort of mortgage for you. It is not enough just to know how the different types work. You need to be able to apply the various advantages and disadvantages of each flavour to your own circumstances, needs and objectives. People get financial planning wrong not because they don't understand how products work, but because they don't spend enough time matching the right product to their own needs.

Finally, some advanced mortgage concepts are analyzed. I will show you how to reduce the length of your mortgage, how to ensure you never get sold the wrong type of mortgage again and how your mortgage can become your new best friend.

They come in lots of different flavours

No two mortgages are the same. If you take a stroll down your typical high street you are bombarded with every type of mortgage under the sun. Banks and building societies advertise their most eye-catching mortgage interest rates in the window to entice new customers. Trying to effectively compare these different rates is an impossible task – it will never be a fair comparison. Apples and oranges spring to mind.

Trying to decide on the 'best' mortgage based on a headline rate is like trying to buy a new car without taking it for a test drive or checking out the engine. All you get to see with mortgage headline rates is the exterior of the product. The really interesting stuff is what happens under the hood. Look a little closer – you might be surprised!

Mortgages differ in two main ways:

■ The type of interest rate
■ The payment method.

There can be other differences as well, but once you understand those that can arise as a result of these two issues, you will be well on your way to getting to grips with mortgages.

Fixed, variable, tracker, discounts, blah, blah, blah

The way your mortgage interest payments work depends on the interest rate structure. For the sake of simplicity there are only two main types, fixed and variable.

Fixed rate

Nice and simple. The interest rate is fixed for a certain length of time, for example six months, two years or ten years. During the period your interest rate is fixed you have absolute certainty that the rate will not change. Even if interest rates at the Bank of England go up to 10% your mortgage payment won't change at all (until the end of the fixed period at least). The downside with a fixed rate is that you won't get to benefit immediately if interest rates go down.

First, fixed rate mortgages are a great idea if you think interest rates might be going up in the near future. Of course the lender is likely to have an expectation of this as well, which means that they will have already taken this likely increase into account when setting their rates. From time to time it is possible to spot discrepancies where bargain basement fixed rates are available even though the interest rates are likely to rise significantly over the next year or two. I always work on the principle that the highly paid economics experts at the bank are likely to know something I don't when I get tempted to second-guess interest rate movements!

Secondly, a fixed rate is often a good idea if you are working to a tight budget and simply cannot afford to have your payments go up for a period of time. The sort of individual in this position would commonly be a newly qualified professional. They may be in a position to meet their monthly mortgage payments as things stand, but if they went up by more than a couple of hundred pounds a month they would be in real financial trouble. While you might miss out on any interest rate drops during your fixed term you do get peace of mind and certainty about this expense.

Variable rates

A variable rate is a mortgage interest rate that can change – it can go up or down. Not only can it go up and down, but it often will. This means that your mortgage payments will vary in line with any changes made to the rate.

You might see this type of interest rate called by a number of different names, including base rate tracker and discount rate mortgages. They all have slight differences but they share very similar qualities.

The base rate tracker does exactly what it says on the tin. It aims to track any changes to the Bank of England base interest rate. A base rate tracker will typically be expressed as a small percentage above the base rate. It will then remain in this position and move to reflect any changes to the base interest rate.

The discount rate is expressed as a discount off the banks' Standard Variable Rate (SVR). Once again, it will change in line with changes made to the SVR. The discount only lasts for a set time. Typically, the shorter the length of the discount, the bigger the discount will be. Three-month and six-month discounted rates are much cheaper than two- or three-year discounted rates.

Interest only or capital repayment?

When you take out a mortgage you will be faced with two main choices – pay your lender just the interest each month or pay back the interest and some of the mortgage capital. The first option is known as an interest only mortgage. The second option is called an interest and capital repayment, or just repayment, mortgage. They are different and will appeal to different people.

There are no right or wrong answers when it comes to making a choice between interest only and repayment mortgages. Both have their good points and bad points. You should make a decision about what works best for you after weighing up all the facts.

I still meet people who are adamant they will never have an interest only mortgage. For them the very idea of only paying off interest is an unacceptable risk. It isn't until I dig a little deeper that I usually discover this is based on a lack of knowledge or real understanding of mortgages and how they work. To be able to make an informed choice about the right sort of repayment option you need to know a little bit more about how these two options work.

Interest only (and capital as well, at the end)

With an interest only mortgage you only pay back the interest. Each and every month your mortgage payment will represent the interest owed for having the mortgage. At the end of your mortgage term, which is agreed at the start when you sign your mortgage contract, you have to repay the entire mortgage amount.

This means that you need to find a way of paying back that really big loan!

Paying back your loan leaves you with two main choices: you can either pay it back by selling your house and using the sale proceeds or by investing your money elsewhere and using this.

The interest only mortgage – sell up and move on

As options go, this one has a certain appeal. If you own a property for long enough you should have a reasonable expectation it will increase in value. You wouldn't want to stake your life on this over a short period (say less than ten years) but you would do this with relative confidence for fifteen-year timeframes or longer.

When the time came for your mortgage to be repaid you could put your house on the market, sell to the highest bidder and use the cash to clear the loan. Because your property would have gone up in value since you bought it there should be some money left over! You could use this to buy somewhere else to live and enjoy your mortgage-free retirement in a smaller property or cheaper area.

While this looks simple on paper, there are some major drawbacks to be aware of:

- **You might not want to move.** Being forced into selling your property might not suit you when the time comes. People form an incredibly strong emotional attachment to their homes. This often starts from the minute the estate agent shows us round for the first time (or in some cases when we read the property details). It often becomes a stronger tie the longer we live somewhere. It is always better to sell your house because you want to rather than being left with no option.

- **It might not be very easy to sell.** Property isn't always the easiest thing to get rid of. At least, you might be able to sell it very easily but selling it at the price you believe it is worth can be a different story. Because there is no certainty about the length of time it will take you to sell, you might have to put your property on the market a year or two before the end of your mortgage. Even then you will not be able to guarantee a timely sale.

■ **Your house might not go up in value.** This whole plan is based on the price of your house going up by the time you have to repay your mortgage. Not only does it have to go up in price, but it has to go up enough to generate the spare cash (in addition to what you need to pay off your mortgage) to buy somewhere else (smaller or in a cheaper area). While we all have a reasonable expectation that our homes will go up in value, we cannot guarantee this will happen. Even if your house does appreciate greatly it might drop again just at the time you need to realize this value. A house is an asset and like any investment its value can go down as well as up.

The interest only mortgage – invest elsewhere

The alternative to selling your house and using the proceeds to repay your mortgage is to use a separate investment vehicle. We go on to talk about investments in more detail in Chapter 06 but I will touch on investing money here as part of the discussion about how this option can work.

If I say the word endowment, you have probably already made a judgement before reaching the end of this sentence. Endowments have been hammered to death in the papers. They are seen as the root of all evil by personal finance journalists who take every opportunity to disparage these mortgage-related investment vehicles.

And yet this is all an endowment is – an investment vehicle many millions of people used with the aim of repaying their interest only mortgage at the end of the mortgage term. An endowment policy also contained an element of life assurance which would repay the entire mortgage in the event that you died before the end of the term.

Endowments went wrong (in some cases) because people didn't really understand how they worked and because they forget to check on progress as time went on. With any long-term investment you are making for a specific purpose it makes absolute sense to check on progress on a regular basis. If you aren't doing this at least once a year then you should be expecting disappointment!

While an endowment might not be your initial choice of mortgage repayment vehicle this general option needs some consideration. The whole point in investing your money to repay your mortgage is the expectation of a greater return from investment than from saving your money in a building society. If you can get superior investment returns (after charges have been taken into account) then it is wise to invest your money. This all means that you have to invest less to get the same result because the investment growth does some of the hard work for you.

Common mortgage questions

There are three main mortgage-related questions that people want to know the answers to:

1 How much can I borrow?

2 What is it going to cost me?

3 How will I pay it back?

The short answers

With these questions there are both short and long versions of the answers. I'll start with the short versions and move on to the more detailed ones a bit later in this chapter:

1 You can borrow as much as a bank, building society or other financial institution is prepared to lend you.

2 At the very least you will have to pay the cost of the interest

on your mortgage each month, and at most you will have to pay the cost of the interest and the repayment of some of the mortgage capital.

3 Either now and throughout the term of the mortgage (if you choose a capital repayment mortgage) or all at the end of the mortgage (if you opt for interest only).

The long versions of the answers are probably a lot more useful.

The long answers

1 How much can I borrow? In the 'old days' it used to be fairly simple to work out how much you could borrow. Mortgage lenders used to work on the basis of multiples of income. They would simply multiply your income by a certain factor and this would then represent the maximum you could have. Add to this your deposit and you were quickly in a position to determine which properties you could afford to buy.

Some lenders still calculate their maximum mortgage lending based on multiples of income. The most generous lenders will probably work on a basis of around three times a single income or 2.75 times joint income. These figures are typical if you have a 5% deposit to offer and an income in the region of £20,000 per annum. Lenders are often prepared to give away more if you have a bigger deposit or a bigger salary. Some will go as far as 4.5 times your joint income if you have a combined or individual gross salary of £60,000 or more.

The new way of doing things has been to move away from multiples and towards affordability as a basis for the calculation. This means that they calculate how big a mortgage you could actually afford to repay based on your monthly disposable income.

One thing that will reduce the maximum amount you will be allowed to borrow is debt. The cost of servicing personal unsecured debt will vastly reduce your ability to get a bigger mortgage. It makes sense to focus your energy and attention on clearing credit card debt and personal loans before making a mortgage application.

2 **What is it going to cost me?** The monthly cost of your mortgage will depend on two main factors – the mortgage interest rate and the length of the mortgage term.

The length of the mortgage can change the amount you have to pay back each month. The longer you have your mortgage for, the less capital you will be paying back each month. This makes the total monthly cost cheaper for a repayment mortgage.

The traditional mortgage term was twenty-five years but these days it is not unusual to see mortgage terms stretching to thirty or even forty years. These longer mortgage terms are made available to make bigger mortgages more affordable.

Remember that the length of your mortgage term is not set in stone. There is nothing to stop you from starting with a forty-year mortgage and then changing this to a twenty-five-year arrangement when you next review your deal. An error that I see some people make is to remortgage after two years but not reduce the mortgage term by the length of time it has already been in place. This means that your mortgage maintains its original term for longer.

If you have an interest only mortgage then the length of the mortgage term is less important. It will still play a role in determining how much money you need to set aside to eventually repay your lender, but it doesn't have an impact on the actual monthly cost of the mortgage deal alone. If you have this sort of mortgage then your monthly cost will essentially be the amount of your mortgage multiplied by the interest rate and divided by twelve.

3 How will I pay it back? The way you pay your mortgage back will very much depend upon whether you choose a repayment or interest only arrangement.

Paying your mortgage back if you have a repayment deal is a very simple affair. Part of what you pay your lender each month will represent a repayment of the mortgage capital. Assuming that you continue to make these payments every month for the term of your mortgage your loan will be fully repaid when it reaches the end date.

You should be aware that a repayment mortgage has a slightly funny 'shape' when it comes to repaying the mortgage capital. In the early years the majority of your monthly payments will consist of interest charges rather than capital repayments. It isn't until the later part of the mortgage term that you start to repay more capital than interest. This occurs because as you pay off more of your capital you get charged less interest, so more of what you pay each month goes towards paying off the capital.

If you have an interest only mortgage then you are faced with choices about how you repay it at the end, some of which is covered above. You can do nothing and sell your property when the mortgage ends, use a separate investment vehicle to create enough capital to repay your mortgage, or pay off lump sums throughout the mortgage term.

If you choose this last option then it is important to make sure that your mortgage lender will not penalize you for doing this. Some mortgage products will allow you to pay off a certain percentage of your mortgage each year without any penalties. Others will treat lump sum payments as a partial redemption of your mortgage and penalize you accordingly. If this is a repayment option you plan to utilize then it is important that you factor this into your mortgage selection criteria.

Getting a mortgage – what does it cost?

When you apply for a mortgage or a remortgage there are, unfortunately, costs involved. These can be broken down into two main parts – the costs involved directly with the mortgage and the costs involved with the property purchase and the legal aspects of this.

The property and legal expenses are more or less unavoidable. For example, you will need to pay a professional adviser to carry out the conveyancing work. Make sure that you work with your conveyancer on a fixed or project fee basis to ensure that costs aren't massively inflated if the purchase becomes more complex or takes longer than originally expected. Also factor in stamp duty and removal costs.

There will also be sums directly attributed to your mortgage. When people shop around for the best mortgage deal they often take a look at the headline rates and little else. The mortgage-related costs should be quite clear as the lender has to disclose them in the Key Facts document you are given before signing on the dotted line. Here are a few of the fees and charges to watch out for:

- Broker fee. Your mortgage adviser may charge you a fee for arranging the mortgage. This is typically expressed as a percentage of the amount of money you are borrowing. Some advisers might charge a fixed fee regardless of the loan size or put a cap on their fee if you are borrowing higher amounts. Other advisers will not charge a fee at all. There is no right or wrong answer when it comes to this fee but you need to be satisfied that you are getting good value for money.
- Booking/arrangement fee. This is the fee that the lender charges you in order to reserve mortgage funds. It is

essentially an administration charge and is often seen if you are applying for a fixed rate mortgage deal.

- **Valuation fee.** This fee covers the cost of the mortgage lender conducting a valuation of the property. They do this to ensure that it is worth enough money to cover their lending if things go wrong. The valuation is not the same as a survey so you will probably need to pay separately for a survey of the property to satisfy yourself that it is in a good condition. Do not base your buying decision on the results of a property valuation as these can often be carried out without the person ever actually seeing the property (known as a desktop valuation). You may also end up having to pay a re-inspection fee if your lender decides that remedial work has to be completed before they will release your mortgage funds.

- **Higher lending charge.** Watch out for this charge. It is there to pay for insurance that only pays out if you cannot keep up your mortgage repayments, leading to your lender having to repossess your house. In the event of this happening and the lender selling the house for less than they have lent you, they can claim on this insurance to cover the loss. It is insurance for the lender and not for you. Many people I know refuse to have a mortgage with this charge in place because it can be very expensive and it offers you, as the borrower, no protection at all.

- **Insurance fee.** If you decide to take out your building insurance with a provider other than your mortgage lender you will typically be charged this small administration fee by the lender. When comparing building insurance quotes make sure you factor this charge into the difference in prices. It is still worth shopping around for the most competitive premiums. Never blindly accept an insurance quote from your mortgage lender without doing some homework first.

- **Bank transfer charge.** If you want to have your mortgage funds moved quickly to complete the property purchase in a timely fashion then you will probably need to pay for a telegraphic transfer to take place.
- **Early repayment charge.** This is another administration charge that is sometimes payable if you repay your mortgage in full.

There are two ways of paying most of these charges. You can either get your chequebook, or you might decide to add some of them on to the amount you borrow from your mortgage lender. Adding charges on to your mortgage might sound like an appealing option, but there are a few things to remember. You are effectively borrowing the amount of these charges from your mortgage lender. Because mortgages tend to have very long terms it will take you many years to fully repay these fees which means you will be charged interest on them.

A little trick that you can use is to ask the lender to add certain charges (such as the booking fee) on to your mortgage and then make use of any available overpayment facility to pay the charges off as soon as the mortgage contract has been completed. This means that you delay paying for an additional fee at what is already bound to be a very expensive time. It also means that if the property purchase falls through for some reason you have not already parted with this money.

Some mortgage mistakes to avoid

Buying a house is probably the biggest financial transaction you will ever undertake in your life. Getting it wrong will feel very bad so here are some of the most common mortgage mistakes you should watch out for and do your best to avoid.

Going to your own bank or building society

When you start thinking about your first mortgage you might feel very tempted to visit your own bank or building society for advice. After all, they know you well (from a financial point of view) and if anyone is going to lend you such a large amount of money it is likely to be them. As a first step, this is one of the biggest mortgage mistakes you need to avoid making.

It's a mortgage mistake to seek advice from your own bank or building society because they are unlikely to have a wide range of products to offer to you. It is very rare for a bank or building society adviser to be 'independent', which means that they will end up recommending a mortgage product from their own very limited range. This means it is less likely to be the most competitive mortgage available and you will end up paying more than you need to.

Don't think for a minute that using another mortgage lender will make life more difficult than getting finance from your existing bank or building society. Every mortgage application is judged on the individual merits of the case so you will need to supply things like bank statements and payslips to support your application. Your independent mortgage adviser will be able to find mortgage deals that you are eligible to apply for based on the financial information you give them.

Using the in-house mortgage advice from your estate agent

As soon as you step into an estate agent's office to start discussing the dream property you are looking for they will almost certainly offer you a free initial consultation with their own in-house mortgage adviser. Mortgage mistake number two is saying 'yes' to this seemingly generous offer.

Some of these in-house advisers have improved their offerings in recent years. Many have become 'independent' and offer mortgage products from the whole of the market. Many still offer only a restricted range of products but with enough scope to have some very competitive deals available for their customers. What really worries me about taking advice from these people is the potential conflict of interest that could exist between the mortgage adviser and the estate agent.

The mortgage adviser should keep everything you discuss with them entirely private and confidential. However, there is a real risk that they might share some confidential information with the firm of estate agents they work with. If they are based in the same office or employed by the same company then that has to be a possibility.

What this means for you, in real terms, is that the estate agent could be put in a stronger position of knowledge about your ability to offer certain amounts of money for property. The higher the offer you make for a flat or house, the more the agent is paid in commission. If they know that you can afford to pay more (based on the information the mortgage adviser has shared with them) this could help them to force your offer up beyond the necessary level, maybe suggesting that the seller of the property holds out for a slightly higher price.

While this might not be happening on a regular basis with every agent and in-house mortgage broker, there is a sure-fire way of ensuring it cannot happen. Use a mortgage adviser who has no connection whatsoever to the agent you are using to purchase the house. This breaks the connection and stops the risk of your agent finding out too much about you.

Living with the Standard Variable Rate (SVR)

When I ask my new clients what interest rate deal they are paying with their existing mortgage lender I always prepare to shudder. At least 80% of the time I find they offer me the same answer – the Standard Variable Rate (SVR).

The SVR is an interest rate for lazy people. It is more expensive than the more competitive rates available to you but mortgage lenders don't worry about this because they know that people very rarely do anything about it.

When you took out your mortgage you probably did a great job. You made sure that you did some shopping around and that the rate you obtained was cheap and competitive. For the first two or three years of your mortgage deal things were probably going very well. And then the day came when your special deal came to an end. Instead of paying a low rate of interest you suddenly found yourself victim of your lender's SVR.

If you discover that you are paying your lender's SVR then it isn't too late to take action. Being on the SVR usually means that there are no redemption penalties for moving to a more competitive provider. Ask your lender for a redemption statement which will show exactly what you would have to pay in the event that you moved to another lender. Armed with that information you can start shopping around for a better deal or, better yet, make an appointment to see an independent mortgage adviser and let them do the running around for you.

The power of offset

The mortgage market has seen a great deal of innovation and development over the last decade. One of the most positive products to come out of this was the offset mortgage.

This type of mortgage works by taking the value of your savings and matching them against what you owe on your mortgage. The amount held in savings cancels out the same level of mortgage capital when it comes to the calculation of interest payments. If you had the same amount in savings as you had as an outstanding mortgage within an offset arrangement, then the two would simply cancel each other out and you would have no interest to pay.

There are a number of benefits to this approach. First, by paying less interest you can repay more of the capital. If you keep up the same total monthly payments then this has the effect of helping you to repay your mortgage faster. Offset mortgages are often used when people want to reduce the term of their mortgage and pay it all back much faster.

The second benefit of using an offset mortgage is the tax advantages. When you earn interest on your savings this is subject to income tax. If you are a higher rate taxpayer you are paying 40% on your savings interest. Even as a basic rate taxpayer you are giving away 20% of your interest as income tax. Offsetting any savings you have against your mortgage removes this income tax liability as there is no interest generated to become subject to tax.

The final benefit of using an offset mortgage is the ability to retain access to your money. The alternative would be to pay off part or your entire mortgage using your savings, but this would mean that you lose control over that money and would not be able to access it again without requesting a further advance on your mortgage. While a mortgage is a long-term financial commitment people often have savings in place for shorter-term financial objectives. This means that you might want to retain access to your money rather than tie it all up in the value of your property.

Some offset mortgages take things a step further. As well as taking your savings into account they can also take your current account into the equation. With this sort of product the interest is calculated on a daily basis to ensure any fluctuation in the balance of your accounts is properly offset against your mortgage. Some people prefer not to take this extra step. Depending on the typical balance of your current account it may not be worthwhile offsetting this source of funds as well.

Opting for offsetting makes sense if you have savings available and you are keen to retain access to these but pay off your mortgage quickly. Be aware that these deals sometimes have a less competitive interest rate than non-offset mortgages, so only go for this option if you plan to really make use of the additional benefits they bring with them.

An alternative strategy

Another financial strategy you need to consider when thinking about your mortgage is renting rather than buying. Renting a property means that you don't benefit from any growth in the value of the property. It also means that you don't lose your money if property prices fall. Renting a property is typically cheaper than buying in the short term. As a tenant you don't have to pay for things like stamp duty or legal fees. Over the longer term there tends to be a stronger argument for buying rather than renting a property. The significant increases in house prices that we have witnessed in recent years might not last for ever but the expectation is still for property to increase in value over any long-term period (ten years or more). Deciding to rent long term rather than buy because you expect house prices to fall is probably a foolish strategy as nobody has a crystal ball. If you want to take a long-term view on house prices then ownership wins hands down over renting.

KEY POINTS

1　By getting to grips with the mortgage basics you can put yourself in a position to make an informed choice when it comes to taking on the biggest financial commitment of your life.

2 You have two main decisions to make when it comes to your mortgage – the type of interest rate and the payment method. The interest rate choice boils down to either a fixed rate or a variable rate (along with some variations on the same theme). You can choose either interest only or capital repayment when it comes to the payment method.

3 If you choose an interest only mortgage then you have to find a way to repay the mortgage when it reaches the end of the term. You could choose to either sell your house and use the proceeds to repay the mortgage or use a separate investment vehicle to build up enough cash to pay it off.

4 The maximum amount you can borrow comes down to your mortgage lender's assessment of how much you can afford to repay. Having any unsecured debt will reduce this borrowing limit so aim to pay off credit cards, store cards and personal loans before making your mortgage application.

5 Always use an independent mortgage adviser to help you find the best mortgage. Every single day there are loads of mortgage deals both entering and leaving the market. Use an independent adviser to do the legwork for you and ensure that you get the most competitive deal going.

6 You can offset your savings against what you owe on your mortgage to reduce what you spend on interest and speed up the repayment of outstanding capital. This approach can reduce your mortgage term and save you income tax on your savings interest.

Plan to protect

> There are worse things in life than death. Have you ever spent an evening with an insurance salesman?
>
> Woody Allen (1935–)

05

Things can go wrong!

You might not plan for it to happen, but a lot can go wrong in life. We cannot always control what happens to us. We can, however, make sure that when the worst does happen it doesn't cause us undue financial hardship.

A good rule to live by to protect your Money Tree from financial disaster is to 'expect the best, but prepare for the worst'.

With a bit of planning it is possible to avoid the financial turmoil that can hit us at any time and from any direction.

What can go wrong?

But just what can go wrong? By understanding the key events that can go wrong you can ensure you are well prepared. There are four main things that can go wrong that you might want to consider protecting your finances against:

- Death
- Critical illness
- Illness or accident
- Medical problems.

Death

As unexpected events go, this first one is pretty bad. It is not a very cheerful subject either! While we all hope for a long and happy life things don't always turn out this way. If you want to protect your Money Tree you have to at least think about death, if only for a few moments.

Before we move on to look at life assurance there is a really important point to make. If you are a single person with no financial dependants then life assurance will either be very low on your list of priorities or even non-existent. If you are in this position then do not be coerced into buying life assurance cover without a very good reason. Plenty of single people I know have been on the receiving end of a heavy sell when it comes to taking out life assurance. It is not a legal requirement to have life assurance in place if you take out a mortgage. Don't be a sales victim. Only get yourself life cover if you need or want it.

If, however, you are in a relationship and/or have children then the emotional impact of death on your nearest and dearest should never be underestimated. The financial impact of an unexpected death can be equally as devastating.

I feel a great deal of cynicism when I hear about how brokers used to sell life assurance products in the 1980s. I'm told that the sales technique of the time was to ask the breadwinner of the house to visualize looking down from above and watching their grieving family. They would be told to picture how, shortly after their tragic death, their partner was unable to keep up mortgage repayments, and then to imagine how they would have to pack their bags and leave the family home as the building society took possession of the property. A powerful sales technique and fortunately not one often used in this day and age, although I'm sure that some less ethical brokers give it a try from time to time.

While this way of doing things has no place in a modern professional advisory business, there is some logic behind it. Asking someone to consider the consequences of their untimely demise is the best way of planning for the unexpected.

Give it a try for yourself. I'm not asking you to shut your eyes and picture someone close to you in tears. I'm asking you to think about the financial consequences of your death for the rest of your family.

There are two main questions that you need to ask yourself at this point:

- What would happen to the financial position of your family if you died tomorrow?
- What would happen if your spouse or partner died tomorrow?

Stop reading this book now, take out a notebook and jot down the numbers. How would your household income change if either event occurred? How much money would the survivor be left with?

Two types of life assurance

Protecting you and your family against the financial impact of death usually involves one of two types of life assurance – term assurance or whole of life assurance.

Term assurance is the simplest form of life assurance there is so it makes an excellent starting point for this subject. It is a type of life assurance that will pay a death benefit (called a sum assured) if you die during a certain period of time. You choose the term when you take out the policy and also select how much you want the sum assured to be.

If you live until the end of the term then the cover stops and the policy finishes. There is no element of investment within a term assurance policy so you don't get any money back if you haven't died before the end of the term. The plus side of this type of policy is that by being pure protection with no investment element it keeps the cost right down.

Term assurance is ideal when you need life assurance cover in place for a known length of time. If you have a mortgage then you may want to ensure it is repaid in full if you die before you have finished paying it back. Term assurance is great for this purpose because there is a known period and you can fit the policy to suit the length of your own mortgage.

Whole of life assurance is a more 'traditional' type of life assurance contract that is rapidly losing its place in the modern world of financial planning. It is a type of policy that will pay out a pre-agreed sum (the sum assured) in the event of your death at any time that the policy is in force. This means that as long as you keep paying the premiums, the cover will stay in place. Unlike term assurance there is no fixed term and the policy can continue for as long as you need it.

Another big difference between term assurance and whole of life assurance is the inclusion of an investment element with the latter. This is the reason that whole of life assurance is increasingly being seen as a dinosaur by modern financial advisers. It doesn't just provide life assurance but also offers an investment plan within the same contract.

The premiums you pay each month for your whole of life assurance are invested in the funds you choose, although most people do not make conscious investment decisions about where they go. In most cases the investment options are limited to some old-style life assurance investment funds. This is not a cutting-edge investment contract.

Some of your investment units within the policy are then 'cancelled' each month to meet the cost of cover. In a lot of cases the premiums you pay for whole of life assurance are subject to a review during the life of the policy. Unlike term assurance they do not stay the same for the term of the policy. A typical review schedule for a whole of life assurance policy might take place for the first time after ten years of owning the policy and then every five years after that.

While I call whole of life assurance a dinosaur it does still play a role in some areas of financial planning, particularly when arranging to pay the cost of inheritance tax for older people. It is generally not suitable, however, for younger people who are looking for straightforward death cover for a specific term or purpose.

Top Tips to slash the cost of your life assurance

While life assurance is quite cheap for young and healthy people with relatively modest protection requirements, it can become a substantial cost for older people, smokers and people who need a lot of life cover. But help is at hand! There are some simple tricks you can use to slash the cost of your life assurance cover. Read on.

1 Review your cover if you haven't done so for a while

The cost of life assurance cover has fallen dramatically over the past five years or so. If you have had some life assurance in place for a while then now is a great time to review it and see what other providers have to offer you. This is particularly true if you originally purchased your cover from a tied agent at your bank or building society. It was unlikely to have been the most competitive cover at the time, and a reassessment of the whole of the market now is extremely likely to throw up a better price for you.

2 Change the basis of the cover to meet your needs

I still meet with clients on a regular basis who have plenty of life cover in place but it is totally inappropriate for their protection needs. It's not unusual to find people who have life cover for their mortgage that ends a couple of years before their mortgage does. Others have life cover in place that is far in excess of what they actually need. In some cases this is because they purchased extra cover many years before when they had extra loans that they have long since repaid.

3 Move from whole of life assurance to term assurance

If you have a specific life assurance protection need, like the protection of a mortgage, then it makes sense to use term assurance rather than whole of life assurance. If you know the actual length of time that you have to cover the risk for then in most cases the cost of term assurance will be much lower than the cost of whole of life assurance. Another plus point is that the premiums will become guaranteed, which makes it much easier to budget for in the future.

Assurance or insurance?

The terms 'assurance' and 'insurance' are often used to describe the various types of protection policy. They sound similar and when said quickly you might even think they are one and the same. But just what are the differences between assurance and insurance?

Assurance is a very traditional word that describes something that assures you something will happen. We often refer to protection policies that pay out on death as life assurance. Death is assured, at some point in the future anyway!

Insurance is a more general word to describe protection policies that are based on events that may or may not occur.

Don't get too hung up on these words. The difference between assurance and insurance is a technical distinction and not something that will cause you to make a bad decision with your money. Leave the worrying to the people who work in the world of insurance (or should that be assurance?).

Lump sum or regular income

When deciding on the best type of life assurance to put in place (if, indeed, you need any) you have to make a decision about the 'shape' of the benefits. Life assurance benefits can be paid in one of two main ways:

- As a lump sum
- As a regular income.

The most traditional route that people tend to choose is to create a lump sum on death. In most cases this makes real sense. If the reason for having the life assurance in place is to repay a liability, like your mortgage, then having a cash sum available to do this is both practical and sensible. However, if your desire for life assurance is more about family security than the repayment of debt, then the structure of a regular income might be worth considering.

Let's assume that you are married and bringing up two young children. You know that you have a financial commitment to your children until they finish full-time education, which could happen when they reach age 21. Once you have ensured that any liabilities would be fully repaid in the event of your death you might want to think about how this ongoing financial commitment would be met until your children finish their studies.

One option to consider is putting in place sufficient life assurance to pay a lump sum that could then be invested or drawn from directly to meet income needs until they reach 21. This option doesn't appeal to a lot of people because it is seen as difficult to manage. Having to budget for the eventual expenditure of a large lump sum of cash is harder than you might initially think!

Critical illness

Having life assurance is great news (financially) for your spouse, children or other financial dependants if you die. If you don't have any of these then many would question the need for life assurance that paid a benefit on your death. You would certainly never see the benefit of this cover and it would not be providing any peace of mind for you during your lifetime.

If you are single with no dependants then a more pressing protection priority might well be to put something in place that paid out in the event that you contracted a critical illness during your lifetime.

When we talk about critical illness we are really referring to the 'Big Three' – heart attack, cancer or stroke. These are the three most common types of critical illness. However, because of advances in and improvements to medical science these illnesses do not always result in death. They may well change your ability to carry out normal activities (like working) or simply change your outlook on what life is all about.

Critical illness insurance provides a lump sum cash benefit that is paid out in the event that you are diagnosed with one of a list of specified critical illnesses. You can opt to add critical illness insurance to a term assurance policy (on either a level or decreasing basis) or a whole of life assurance policy.

A word of warning at this stage – critical illness cover can be expensive. It costs much more than the equivalent level of life assurance, simply because the risk of you making a claim during your lifetime is higher than the risk of you dying. This is particularly true for women who have a better life expectancy than men but a much higher chance of being diagnosed with a critical illness.

If someone is trying to sell you a critical illness policy they will probably throw some of the following statistics at you. For example, did you know that there is a one in three chance of suffering from cancer at some point during your life? This statistic is often used to convince people of the need to purchase critical illness cover.

You might also be told how more than 260,000 people have a heart attack each and every year. The life insurance salesman might even explain to you that one in four women and one in five men will be a victim of a stroke at some stage in their life.

These statistics can actually be fairly misleading because they apply to the whole of your lifetime, and eventually everybody suffers from something! The chances of contracting a critical illness earlier in your life is much lower than it is during your 'autumn years'. It is also fair to say that the financial implications of cancer, for example, at 80 years old is very different from getting it during your 30s or 40s.

I take a slightly different approach when it comes to recommending this type of cover. While I agree that there is a risk that everyone will suffer a critical illness during their lifetime, I think that this has to be taken in perspective and viewed alongside the risk of other events occurring. To insure against every risk you might face in life would be prohibitively expensive. What you need to do, therefore, is prioritize the risks you face and decide on which ones would have the biggest financial impact. You may only be able to afford to meet the costs of the first item on your list, or maybe just the top three. What really matters is that you have established what the risks are and decided on how you plan to address them.

Illness or accident

There is a fate worse than death for a lot of people, and that is not being able to work (and earn an income) for a long period of time as a result of sickness or injury. In fact, this can have a more profound effect on your personal financial planning than dying!

We all have regular financial commitments to meet and most people do this from regular income we earn from employment or self-employment. If that stream of income gets switched off then we might be able to 'tough it out' for a few months or so. Earlier we talked about the need for an emergency savings fund that would see us through a few months if the worst were to happen.

Getting through a few months of lost income is a very different problem to getting through a year or more of zero income (other than the minimal State benefits you might receive). Not only would this prevent you from meeting your monthly committed spending requirements (including your mortgage payments) but it would also have a serious impact on your ability to plan for the future. Future savings, investments and retirement plans would have to be immediately placed on hold if your income stopped.

There is a solution to consider.

Income protection insurance is a very simple type of protection policy. To understand how it works it is important to know about the different parts of protection:

- The length of time it takes for this type of policy to pay you a benefit will depend on something called the **deferred period**. This is the length of time you agree when you take out the policy before any benefits are paid out to you. The longer the deferred period you select, the cheaper the cost of cover. If you go for a very short deferred period then the cost of cover will become more expensive.

- **You decide if you want the benefit to be paid weekly, monthly or annually.** You get to choose how often you would need to receive the money, but in most cases you would elect for it to be paid monthly in line with your monthly financial commitments.

- You decide when you take out this sort of policy **how much cover you need.** The more cover you ask for, the more expensive the premiums become.

There is a limit on how much cover you are allowed to have in place with income replacement insurance. This is because the company that offers the insurance is worried that you won't have an incentive to get back to work if the benefit is too high. By setting the maximum benefit at a level that will allow you to pay for the things you need to pay for but not the things you want, you are likely to be more motivated to get back on your feet and back to your job.

The highest level of cover you can have is typically set at 60% of your earnings (before tax is deducted).

- **The premium is what you pay to have cover in place.** Premiums can come in many different shapes and sizes. Some are called 'guaranteed'. This means that once you get offered a premium it will stay the same for the rest of the policy. Other premiums could be 'reviewable' and are subject to change after a certain length of time. This makes the cost of having cover in place less predictable and harder to budget for, but it could result in the premiums starting off cheaper than guaranteed premiums for an equivalent policy.

A number of factors will influence how much you will have to pay for income replacement insurance. These include how much cover you want, how old you are, your medical history (and the medical history of close relatives), how long you will wait before benefits are paid (the deferred period) and if you are a man or a woman. If you are a woman then you will have to pay more for the equivalent level of cover of a man because, in general terms, while women live longer than men, they are more likely to be seriously ill during their lifetime.

Before putting any income replacement insurance cover in place you should check with your employer to find out what they already provide within your contract. From experience I can tell you that some companies are better than others when it comes to this benefit. Some will only continue to pay you for the absolute minimum length of time before falling back on statutory sick pay. Others will keep up your income payments for much longer, or maybe reduce them to half their normal level after a given length of time.

Medical problems

In the UK we are extremely fortunate to have a National Health Service (NHS) that offers a 'free' service covered by the cost of our National Insurance contributions. In fact, in a serious medical emergency most people would agree that the NHS does a fantastic job of getting us patched up and back on our feet again.

However, there are perceived to be some serious problems with the NHS when it comes to other forms of medical treatment. The time it takes to see a specialist or have an operation when we have a non-life threatening condition is often longer than we would accept as convenient.

One way of getting this treatment faster is to pay and 'go private'. This option is often beyond the financial reach of most people, but with a little bit of planning and the use of private medical insurance (PMI) it can become a viable option.

PMI is a type of protection policy that is designed to meet the costs of private medical treatment. It allows you to get treatment much faster and at private rather than public medical facilities. The speed of treatment is particularly important if you are self-employed and cannot afford the business implications of having to wait a long time to receive treatment or an operation.

The cost of PMI does not come cheaply. As with all insurance the insurer has to consider the risk they are taking on board and charge for it accordingly. Most policies will exclude any pre-existing medical conditions that you have, at least for a certain period of time. This prevents you from claiming for a medical condition you already had or knew about when you took the policy out.

PMI policies may also carry other exclusions that are designed to ensure that the provider is not left paying out benefits for a pro-longed period of time. This is one type of protection policy where it really pays to read the small print and check that you are comfortable with any exclusions or conditions being imposed before you sign on the dotted line.

The amount you pay for PMI will depend on a number of factors. These include your age, gender and current state of health. Even the area in which you live may have an influence over the cost of your PMI. There are some ways of keeping the cost of cover as low as possible. First, offer to pay a higher excess. This is the amount of money that you have to pay personally before any benefits are paid out. Another way of keeping the cost down is to set the policy up on a group rather than individual basis. Group PMI is significantly cheaper than an individual PMI policy. Check with your employer to see if they would consider setting up a group PMI policy and then charging you individually for the cost of the premiums.

How much cover do I need?

Deciding what type and level of protection you and your family need is actually quite a difficult task. There is no precise science behind working out an adequate level of protection. In fact, financial planning in general is more of an art than a science. While this means that there might not be any 'right' answers it does not stop there from being lots of 'wrong' answers!

A very general guide to the situations where varying types of protection policy might be appropriate follows. This is a broad guide rather than tailored advice, but hopefully it will help you to see how different policies can work in different situations.

1 If you have an interest only mortgage then you might consider level term assurance if you want to make sure it is fully repaid in the event of your death. You could set the policy term to finish when your mortgage is due to be repaid. The sum assured would need to be at least the same level as your out-standing mortgage balance.

2 If you have a capital repayment mortgage then decreasing term assurance might be a better choice for you. This is because the sum assured will reduce in line with the mortgage capital that is left to pay. As you make mortgage repayments you will be reducing the balance and your need for life assur-ance will be decreasing at the same time. However, some people still prefer to choose a level term assurance policy for use in conjunction with their capital repayment mortgage. This gives them a bit of additional life cover, with the gap between the cover needed and the cover provided actually growing over the term of the mortgage.

3 If your employer will pay you full salary for six months in the event of incapacity and then nothing you might want to con-sider getting some income replacement insurance with a six-month deferred period. This means that no benefits would be

paid from the insurance policy until your employer stopped paying you. Having a longer deferred period also makes this type of insurance cheaper, so always find out how long your boss will pay you for before taking out any kind of income replacement insurance. You can tailor the income replacement insurance to fit your existing benefits from employment. Remember that you are looking for harmony when it comes to growing your Money Tree.

4 If you are self-employed you might consider private medical insurance. This would ensure that you would not have to wait a long time for surgery or an important medical consultation on the NHS. Having private medical insurance is often a priority for people who are self-employed because they want to get back on their feet quickly in the event of medical problems.

KEY POINTS

1 **Four main things can go wrong and have a substantial impact on your finances – death, critical illness, illness or accident, and medical problems.** You can plan to protect your finances against all of these risks, but first you need to understand what the impact of each would be and give them a priority in your financial plans.

2 **Death is an easy risk to plan for by putting an appropriate type and level of life assurance protection in place.** Your choice of life assurance will consist of two main options – term assurance or whole of life assurance. The most appropriate type of life assurance will depend upon the risk you are trying to cover.

3 **Financial protection from the impact of contracting a critical illness can often be a higher priority than life assurance if you have no financial dependants, and even if you do have a spouse**

and/or children it can be important. This type of protection is often very expensive so it is important to understand where this risk comes in terms of your financial priorities.

4 An illness or accident leading to the loss of your income can have a more serious financial impact on your Money Tree than death. Not only does it mean you cannot meet committed expenditure but it also places a hold on your ability to plan for the future. You can use income replacement insurance to plan for this risk but it is important to tailor this type of cover to fit in with any existing benefits you have in place from your employment.

5 Getting medical treatment promptly can be essential to the health of your Money Tree, particularly if you are self-employed. The cost of private medical treatment is often prohibitive but it is possible to use private medical insurance to cover this risk. Always read the small print to understand which terms and exclusions apply to the policy. It is better to know this now than when you come to make a claim.

6 Deciding how much cover you need to have in place is more of an art than a science. Start by running through a variety of financial scenarios and work out what the impact of each risk looks like. From this starting point you should be able to establish the amount of money you and/or your family would need to receive to ensure the continued growth of your Money Tree.

Intelligent investment

> Never invest your money in anything that eats or needs repairing.
>
> Billy Rose (1899–1966)

06

Investing money can be a source of major disappointment. People often take it really badly if an investment loses money, or does something else unexpected. If they invested through an adviser or broker of some kind, that person will also often find themselves being blamed, regardless of how many times the risk warning was shown, highlighting that investments can fall in value. However much we're told that they carry a risk, the possibility that we really could lose or not gain money never seems to properly sink in.

There is an unbreakable and irrefutable relationship between risk and reward when it comes to investment. This means that if you want more reward you have to be prepared to take more risk. Of course everyone would love an investment that offered maximum reward for zero risk, but this is simply not possible. There is something known as the 'efficient frontier' which prevents this from taking place. It is like a glass ceiling that forces you up the risk spectrum for every extra bit of reward you try to achieve with your money. Breaking the efficient frontier glass ceiling is impossible. Yet people are still wooed into thinking it might be possible. Is this down to greed or simply a lack of understanding?

Getting the investment branch of your Money Tree correct isn't rocket science. It is just a case of research and understanding. If you invest your money based on a whim or a snippet of information you have heard on the golf course, you are on the fast track to disappointment.

Over the last few years we've seen a rise in 'fad' investment. This often includes the classic property investment junkies, usually enticed into some unbelievable investment 'opportunity' at an introductory seminar. These property seminars always make people rich, but they are usually those standing on the stage and collecting your membership fees.

The main reason for investing money is to make it grow faster than it would have done if you held it in cash. To make it grow faster you have to take some risk. The faster you want it to grow, the more risk you have to take. However, the risks of investing in some 'unmissable opportunities' are too great – if it sounds too good to be true, it probably is.

This chapter will explain how to make sure you grow a healthy investment branch for your Money Tree. By demystifying terms such as 'risk', 'reward', 'volatility' and 'asset allocation' I will teach you to follow a tried and tested investment process that will help you take control of your investments and stop taking unnecessary risks with your money.

The value of your investments may go down as well as up

You might have seen this classic risk warning before – on TV, in the newspaper, on billboards at railway stations – and heard it on the radio. When you invest your money you expose it to risk.

Risk comes in four different shapes and sizes:

- **Risk to your capital.** The value of the money you invest can go down in value. With some forms of investment your money can disappear completely.
- **Risk to your income.** The level of income that comes from your investment can drop.
- **Shortfall risk.** There is a risk that your investments will not meet your objectives or targets.
- **Inflation risk.** There is a danger that the value of your money will not keep pace with the rate of inflation. The purchasing power of your money will be eroded by its effects.

Most investors only consider the risk to their capital, probably the easiest type to measure. Say you invest £1,000 in shares, buying 100 of them at £10 each, and you see the value of those shares go down to £8 each as the company hits a rocky patch: it's very clear that your original £1,000 is now only worth £800 and it feels very important to you. However, you mustn't forget income risk, shortfall risk and inflation risk because they all play an important role in the amount of money you are (or are not) generating.

Shortfall risk is the risk that your investments will not reach their original target – the amount you needed them to grow to by a certain date to meet your financial objective. Not everyone has targets when they invest money. For many investors the simple prospect of getting a better return than they would have received in the bank or building society is a good enough motivation to take additional risk. Other investors will set very specific targets. For example, if you are using an investment to repay your interest only mortgage then the shortfall risk is that your investment will not be worth enough to repay the mortgage.

The easiest way to reduce shortfall risk is by regular monitoring and review. By checking up on your investments on at least an annual basis you can establish the likelihood of the plan meeting your target. You can also take corrective action to reduce the likely shortfall, such as increasing the amount you invest each month.

Most investments produce an income as well as giving the investor the prospect of some capital growth. If you invest in shares then this income is called 'dividends'. For a property investor it is rental income. If you are dependent on your invest-ments for all or part of your income then income risk is the risk that the level of this income will fall below your required level. This is particularly relevant for retired people who have limited sources of money. Income risk should be a greater concern for you if you rely heavily on your investments for your income.

Inflation is the rising cost of goods and services over time. For example, just think back ten years to the cost of petrol. Inflation is often measured by changes to the Retail Prices Index (RPI), a basket of goods and services that are supposed to represent the things a typical household would regularly buy.

Inflation risk refers to the risk that your money will not keep pace with these rising costs. This means that over time the purchasing power or 'real' value of your investments is being eroded. We are currently experiencing a period of very low inflation so this type of risk is less of a worry for most investors, but if inflation reaches double figures again in the future it will become a more pressing investment consideration.

What is my investment risk profile?

Take this quick quiz to give yourself a general indication of how much risk you would feel comfortable taking with your money.

1 How much do you know about investments?

   a Nothing at all.

   b The same as most people.

   c I'm an investment guru.

2 If you had invested £1,000 and it dropped in value by 30% in one day, what would you be inclined to do?

   a Cut my losses and sell the remaining investments.

   b Do nothing.

   c Invest more in the same funds.

3 When you make a big financial decision how do you normally feel about it afterwards?

   a Terrible – I have sleepless nights worrying if I have made the right decision.

   b Just a little bit concerned but generally okay.

   c Extremely confident about the choices I have made.

4 Which of the following investments would you be most tempted to pick?

   a An average of 4% growth each year with no negative returns in the last ten years.

   b An average of 9% growth each year but a loss of up to 3% once every three years.

   c An average of 14% growth each year but with losses of up to 8% every two years.

5 For what length of time are you prepared to invest your
   money?

   a Up to five years
   b Five to ten years
   c Over ten years

Mostly As – you have a fairly cautious risk profile.
Mostly Bs – you take a more moderate view of investment risk.
Mostly Cs – you have an adventurous attitude towards
   investment risk, reward and volatility.

But risk and reward isn't just about risk and reward! To really get
to know investments you also have to consider the third element. When I talk to my clients about investing money I always
talk about the relationship between risk, reward and *volatility*.

The motion of the ocean

Talking about risk and reward doesn't present the whole picture.
When we consider investment risk we should always refer to the
relationship between risk, reward and volatility. Volatility is the
up and down movement of the value of an investment. Higher
risk investments tend to be more volatile. They tend to rise and
fall more sharply in value than lower risk investments.

Volatility is just like wave movement in the ocean. Low risk and
low volatility investments are a bit like a calm ocean. A higher
risk investment is like being in a boat on very choppy water.

There is nothing wrong with a volatile investment when you are
prepared to take higher risks and when you have enough time for
your investments to recover from a 'dip in the waves'. Planning

your investments for retirement is a good example here. Investing money within a pension fund often means a relatively well-known timescale. Everyone has a good idea of when they would ideally like to retire and it becomes easy then to plan your investments for this anticipated retirement age.

If you have a very long term to this retirement age then volatility shouldn't be too much of a concern. While it is never nice to see the value of your pension fund fall on paper, you at least have the time left for the investments to recover before you need to use them. The closer you get to your planned retirement date, the more likely it is you want less volatility in your pension fund. If you have only a few years before your retirement then it is unlikely you want to see the value of your pension leaping around all over the place. It is more likely that you want to see steady and predictable investment returns instead.

If we are in agreement that volatility is just as important as risk and reward (and in fact, the three are linked) then it is time to move on to the next investment concept of this branch of the Money Tree – pound cost averaging.

Buy low, buy high, but always keep buying

When the value of your investments fall the natural instinct for more cautious investors is to sell their holdings and stop making future investments. After all, who wants to invest money in a falling investment market?

The intelligent investor loves a falling market because it means cheaper investments. The cheaper the investments are, the more you can buy with the same amount of money.

When you invest money regularly (e.g. monthly) you will sometimes buy your investments cheaply and sometimes at a more expensive price. When the market has fallen your same pound will buy you more 'units' than it did the month before when the price of each unit was higher. This means that when the market rises again you will own more investment units at the higher price.

For example, say you invest £100 each month in an investment fund. In month one the price per unit might be 10p and you become the proud owner of 1,000 units. In month two the market has risen and each unit is worth 15p. Your original investment (from month one) is now 1,000 units at 15p and is therefore worth £150, but your £100 investment this month will only buy 666 units at this new price. So you now have 1,666 units. In the third month the market takes a dive and the value of each investment unit is only 5p. You are already the proud owner of 1,666 units, but they are now only worth 5p each – a disappointing total of £83.30. However, at the new low price of 5p per unit your £100 monthly investment will buy you 2,000 units. Your total number of units is now up to 3,666. So, when the market recovers to 12p per unit in month four, the total value of your portfolio (in which you have invested £300) is now £439.92.

This example shows how pound cost averaging can work. A more volatile investment market can mean more frequent low prices (buying opportunities) as well as high prices. By continuing to invest your money on a regular basis, some months you will buy more units while others you will buy fewer units.

It's all about asset allocation

The best Money Tree investment has very little to do with opening the Sunday paper and picking out an advertisement for a top-performing fund. Making your investment decisions based on past performance is a sure-fire way to consistently invest in bad or 'dog' funds. This method will often leave you out in the cold. What you *do* need to do is make sure you have a good asset allocation for your investment. This means spreading your investment across the different asset classes.

But just what is an 'asset class'?

There are four main asset classes:

1 Cash
2 Fixed interest securities
3 Property
4 Equities (shares).

Each asset class is very different and each behaves in very different ways.

Cash, for example, usually offers a very stable capital value (it doesn't go up and down in price) but it offers the lowest return of all of the asset classes over the medium to long term. Equities are much more volatile, particularly over the shorter term, but they offer the greatest potential for long-term returns.

These differences are what make asset allocation crucial to a good investment decision. Because each asset class acts in a different way it is essential to hold the right amount of each one in your investment portfolio.

Most people pick funds without giving any consideration to asset allocation but when you invest money you are always making an asset allocation decision. Some investors make this decision consciously and others don't give it a second thought. You should start paying more attention to asset allocation when making your investment decisions.

Research has shown that up to 90% of the difference in investment performance comes down to asset allocation decisions rather than fund or stock selection. If you think about this for a moment it makes perfect sense. Let's assume that you have picked the top-performing UK equity investment fund. You might be pretty pleased with yourself but if the entire UK equity sector is going down in value then all you have managed to do is lose less money than you would have done investing in an average or poorly performing fund. In fact, it's more likely that you will choose an average fund than a 'good' fund. This just compounds the problem.

By allocating your investments to the main asset classes you will have exposure to investments that are doing different things – when one asset class is going down in value another should be on the rise, and vice versa.

Those who take care over their asset allocation are intelligent investors. They have a strong branch of their Money Tree because they understand what each asset class consists of.

What does each asset class involve?

Each asset class is different. To understand investment you have to be able to understand how each asset class works and what types of investments fall into each category. The following acts as a brief introduction to each of the three remaining investment asset classes, with cash already covered on pages 56–72.

Fixed interest securities

This asset class contains two main types of investments – gilts and corporate bonds. Gilts are debt issued by the British Government and they are considered to be very secure (because they are backed by the State). They only offer very modest returns over the medium to longer term but they should be considered as part of a wider investment portfolio because they are relatively stable and behave in a very different way to equities.

Corporate bonds are another form of debt but they are issued by companies rather than the Government. This makes them more speculative than gilts but, as a result, they should pay a better return to investors to compensate for this additional risk.

Property

When we talk about property in respect of investment we are usually referring to commercial rather than residential property. This means shops, offices and warehouses. Some property funds invest directly in 'bricks and mortar' but others will invest in the shares of property companies. Property as an asset class offers relatively low risk to capital value, although like all investments this can go down. The value of property behaves quite differently to the value of equities so it is important to hold some of this asset class in a well-diversified investment portfolio.

Equities

Equities means shares in companies. As the owner of part of the company you are entitled to two parts of an investment – any change in the capital value of the shares (i.e. if the share price increases, you'll make money if you sell your shares) and also any dividend income paid out by the company. Dividends are normally paid in two or more instalments during the course of the year. In some cases they can be quite paltry amounts but some companies place a greater emphasis on dividend payments to shareholders.

Equities represent the highest risk asset class but also offer the best potential for long-term capital growth. You can further divide this asset class into different geographical regions (e.g. the UK or US) and different sectors within the region. Investing in non-UK equities introduces an additional risk to the melting pot – currency fluctuation. As well as the value of the investment going down you also have to contend with the possibility that the currency exchange rate could move against you.

Investing directly in equities is not for the faint-hearted. Because you are investing in a single asset class and probably a limited number of companies within that class, you are not spreading your investment so very little diversification is taking place. This means that if this class is having a tough time or if the companies you have chosen to invest in are falling in value you will be losing money. To invest in equities directly you need to find yourself a stockbroker and there is no shortage of these on the internet. Internet share dealing has driven down the cost of buying stocks and shares as well as making it easier to conduct research on the companies you are interested in investing with.

There is no secret to intelligent investment

Investing money intelligently isn't incredibly difficult. It is, however, more of an art than a science. I am yet to see a convincing scientific model that will guarantee high investment returns with little or no risk to the capital. When I see 'sure-fire investment techniques and methods' being promoted I'm always a little sceptical.

I have seen a great number of financial 'artists' who seem to have natural instincts when it comes to investment.

Around three years ago I was taught the intelligent way to invest money. I now use this process on a daily basis with some very wealthy clients. It works well for two main reasons:

- **It has a clear structure.** My process is a route map for investment from A to Z. It is easy to follow each stage in the process.
- **It helps to manage expectations.** When you invest your money there is nothing worse than being promised one thing and receiving another.

1 Set clear objectives

There is no point in investing your money and exposing it to risk unless you have good reason for doing so. Be very clear about why you want to make an investment. You need to decide whether you want to achieve growth in the value of your money, an income from your investment, or a bit of both. You also need to have a timescale in mind.

2 Determine risk

Before lifting an investment finger you have to decide how much risk you feel comfortable taking with your money. Just because you are going to invest doesn't mean that you have to take high levels of risk. Spend time thinking about your attitude towards investment risk, reward and volatility. Don't allow yourself to be pigeonholed into a particular risk definition without due consideration.

3 Strategic asset allocation

This is the high-level decision you make about allocating your money to the main asset classes. At this level you might decide to invest 30% in property, 20% in fixed interest securities, 45% in equities and 5% in cash. This becomes your long-term (or strategic) asset allocation model and you should return your portfolio to this original position each year.

4 Tactical asset allocation

This is the small tweaks and changes you make to your asset allocation model to reflect the short-term expectations you might have about the investment market. For example, if you think that property is going to shoot up in value over the next twelve months you might change your exposure to this asset class from 30% to 35% for the first year. This stage in the investment process is all about making subtle changes to your portfolio rather than backing one horse.

5 Tax wrapper selection

Until this stage we haven't given any thought to 'products', only 'investment'. Now it is time to choose a product or 'tax wrapper' to minimize tax on your investment and this decision will normally be driven by your attitude towards personal taxation. For example, you might decide to invest within an ISA, investment bond or even directly without using a tax wrapper at all.

6 Fund selection

Once you know which tax wrapper you are opting for it is time to select the specific investments. You need to pick and choose investment funds to fill the asset allocation model you have built.

7 Benchmarking and review

This is the remedy to the 'fire and forget' investment portfolios that always lead to disappointment. First, benchmarking means establishing a form of measurement so you can judge the relative success (or failure) of your investment portfolio over time. This also helps you to keep a handle on risk. The review part of this stage means putting a note in your diary for three, six or twelve months' time to sit down and see how things are going. It doesn't make sense to monitor your investments on a much more frequent basis than this. You will only end up reacting to short-term changes in value when your focus should be on the bigger picture.

How do you actually invest your money?

When it comes to actually making an investment for the first time you have two main choices – either invest directly, or indirectly using collective investment funds. For the first-time investor it makes more sense to choose the latter option. Direct investment requires a high level of knowledge and confidence. You also need significant amounts of money to make this a cost-effective method, especially if you want to diversify the investments and manage risk.

Collective investment funds are a more practical and attractive option for the majority of investors. Essentially you pool your money with other investors into much bigger investment funds. These funds are run by professional managers that go to the market and invest in individual shares, properties and fixed interest securities.

Collective investments are available to cover all of the main asset classes and each has a specialist focus. You can even choose funds that are designed to match your risk profile. These 'managed' funds are a good idea if you are starting off with a small investment (say £50 a month) as the fund manager will do the asset allocation for you within their fund. It is worth keeping a close eye on the make-up of a managed fund both when you make the investment and then again on a regular basis. They can change quite dramatically over the course of time.

ISA magic

ISA is probably one of the most commonly used acronyms in the world of financial services. These three little letters stand for Individual Savings Account – a tax-efficient wrapper for your investments. We've already talked about using a Mini Cash ISA in Chapter 03. Think of an ISA as a tax-resistant suit of armour in which to keep your cash or investment funds. They come in a few different shapes and sizes, but all have similar elements.

There are certain rules about which ISAs you can have and how much you can put into this tax-efficient arena. In simple terms, each tax year you can have:

- One Maxi ISA, or
- One Cash Mini ISA and one Stocks & Shares Mini ISA.

You can't have a Mini and a Maxi ISA in the same tax year. It's not allowed and it causes all sorts of problems when the tax department eventually finds out (and it will!).

The only other type of ISA you might occasionally hear reference to is the TESSA Only ISA (or TOISA). These are able to accept the capital built up in the old Tax Exempt Special Savings Accounts (TESSA). They work a bit like a Cash ISA but can only be used by people who have built up money using the old TESSA system which came to an end in 1999.

Either the Mini or the Maxi route enables you to invest up to £7,000 each tax year in total, but in slightly different combinations. The Maxi ISA is straightforward – you can put up to £7,000 in this during a single tax year. The Mini ISA comes in two different flavours – cash and stocks and shares. With the cash version you can invest up to £3,000 and the stocks and shares variety lets you invest up to £4,000.

When I hear people talk about ISAs and tax efficiency I always suggest that they pause for breath and look at the tax advantages with a fresh pair of eyes.

There are three main types of tax to try to reduce or remove when it comes to investing your money – income tax, capital gains tax and inheritance tax. I've covered each of these in Chapter 02 so I won't cover this again here.

The most likely order of priority when it comes to tax-efficient investment will usually run in the same order. The following is my tax-efficient investment shopping list. Income tax first, because it has the most immediate impact on the value of your investments. Capital gains tax is then best avoided when you come to sell your investments. This includes the times when you need to switch between certain investments. Inheritance tax falls lower in the order of priorities because it doesn't hit your estate until you die.

ISAs are pretty good at sheltering your cash or investments from items one and two on our shopping list, but terrible at item number three.

Income tax has to be paid on any income from your investments, including interest on cash in the bank. If you have £3,000 in a Cash Mini ISA you get any interest gross rather than net. This means that you prevent your interest from suffering 10%, 20% or 40% income tax, depending on which tax bracket you fall into because of other earnings.

This should be a relatively easy decision for most people to make. If you have cash in a bank or building society and the interest is being taxed at between 10% and 40%, it makes perfect sense to shelter up to £3,000 of this in a Cash ISA. Assuming the headline interest rate is 5.0% on both the bank account and the ISA, and that you can afford to save £3,000 in the latter, a higher rate taxpayer gets interest of £90 from the bank account (after income tax) or £150 from the ISA. That's an extra £60 a year just for moving your money from one place to another. For a basic rate taxpayer the benefits are still significant – a £30 improvement for making use of the ISA allowance.

While this might not seem like huge money today, consider the effect of using the £3,000 Cash ISA allowance every year for, say, five years. The effect of adding £3,000 a year to a tax-efficient savings environment soon adds up. Compound returns on gross interest will lead to much greater funds than compound returns on interest paid after income tax has been deducted.

Investment income from stocks and shares works in a slightly different way to interest on savings. Since April 2004 it hasn't been possible for an ISA manager to reclaim the 10% tax credit paid on dividend income. Calling it a tax credit is a bit misleading. It's actually 10% income tax, and the rules introduced in 2004 mean that income from shares paid into an ISA are received after this has been taken off. Even as a non-taxpayer you can't reclaim the income tax charge on this type of investment income. However, higher rate taxpayers don't have to worry about more income tax being taken from them if they hold their stocks and shares inside an ISA.

For this reason Stocks & Shares ISAs are only income tax efficient for higher rate taxpayers or investors in fixed interest investments – gilts and corporate bonds. The income received on this type of investment is completely free of income tax when held within an ISA. Because of this it is best not to let the tax tail wag the investment dog if you are considering an ISA investment. Tax efficiency is important but it should not be the main reason for making an investment.

Investment gains within an ISA are completely free of capital gains tax. This doesn't matter when it comes to the Cash ISA where there are no investment gains to deal with (only interest income). For most people, it doesn't really matter for Stocks & Shares ISAs either. While these are capable of making investment gains for the majority of people they will not exceed the level of our annual CGT exemptions. Each and every year we are all entitled to receive a certain level of capital gains on our investments without them being subject to CGT. For the 2006/07 tax year this exemption was £8,800.

All of this means that for a basic rate or nil-rate income taxpayer investing in equities who hasn't made use of their annual CGT allowance, an ISA could be considered as a bit of a waste of time from a tax saving point of view. One advantage that remains, and often has a high level of appeal, is that you don't have to declare investment income or gains on your tax return each year. It means one less figure to worry about.

Going green

When it comes to investing money one of the more popular requests I have from clients these days is ethical or socially responsible investment (SRI). 'Going green' is becoming big in the world of personal finance and it is important not to ignore the potential (and risks) this area of investment can represent.

There are currently over 100 socially responsible pension and investment funds available in the UK. The popularity of these 'ethical' investment funds has grown rapidly since the launch of the first fund around twenty years ago.

The widening availability of such funds is a direct result of the demand from investors who want to make sure that they are doing the right thing with their money. For a person who is ethical and socially responsible in other aspects of their day-to-day life, pensions and investments can pose a dilemma.

Because of the way collective investments work (with a fund manager selecting lots of individual stocks) it can be difficult to establish the intentions of these companies. Socially responsible investment offers the individual an opportunity to make a difference to the world with their pension funds and lump sum investments.

How are socially responsible investment funds run?

No two socially responsible investment funds are the same. Each of them uses different methods for determining the most appropriate holdings to select. Therefore it is important to understand the methodology behind the fund to ensure it meets your needs as an ethical or socially responsible investor.

The screening process used is essential to ensure that the companies in which the fund manager chooses to invest are suitable for your ethical investment needs.

Ethical screening takes place at two levels. The first is the negative level. This eliminates any undesirable companies from the fund manager's list of potential investments. The second is the positive level. The fund manager looks for positive attributes within companies in which they are considering making an investment.

What are the risks?

As I've explained earlier in this chapter, there are four main types of investment risk: capital risk, shortfall risk, income risk and inflation risk. The capital risk involved with socially responsible investment is sometimes considered to be higher than for other types of investment.

Because of the screening process often employed by fund managers these investments tend to be focused on a much narrower range of stocks. This lack of diversification can lead to higher levels of capital risk.

It is also often the case that the most socially responsible companies are smaller companies. There is more capital risk involved in investing in smaller companies than larger companies.

However, risk can be identified and managed. Depending on your own attitude to investment risk, reward and volatility an appropriate investment portfolio can be designed that takes your ethical considerations into account. By selecting the appropriate mix of investment assets an independent financial adviser can recommend investments that will meet your risk and reward requirements.

KEY POINTS

1 The link between risk and reward is both clear and unbreakable. You cannot get more of the latter without taking more of the former. Anyone who offers you high investment return without risk should be treated with a healthy dose of cynicism.

2 There is more than one type of investment risk. As well as taking capital risk into account you also have to consider income, shortfall and inflation risk. These may or may not matter much to you, but you should be aware that they exist for all investments.

3 Higher risk investments are often more volatile than lower risk opportunities. Volatility is not a problem if you are investing money for a long period but it becomes less appealing if you don't have the time for your money to recover in value. By investing money regularly you can take advantage of this volatility by occasionally investing your money when prices are lower.

4 Asset allocation is much more important than selecting top performing funds. There are four main asset classes – cash, fixed interest, property and equities. Each asset class behaves in a different way so the secret to intelligent investment is getting the right asset class mix for your individual objectives.

5 Intelligent investment involves following a tried and tested process – identifying your objectives and risk, strategic asset allocation, tactical asset allocation, selecting a tax wrapper, choosing funds, benchmarking and review.

6 Using an ISA can be tax efficient for some investors but don't overplay the value of these tax benefits as they can be less important for some people.

7 Socially responsible investment has become a more popular investment choice in recent years but it means different things to different investors. No two 'green' funds are the same so you need to look at the fine detail. SRI can involve greater investment risk because of the screening process and focus on smaller companies.

A financially secure retirement

> When a man retires, his wife gets twice the
> husband but only half the income.
>
> Chi Chi Rodriguez (1935–)

07

A real story

So there I was, in a soundproof room in London late on a Sunday evening. I'd just driven for over two hours to appear as a guest on a personal finance radio show. As I was sitting there with the microphone just inches from my mouth and the red 'on air' light illuminated I started to realize what I was letting myself in for. This was a consumer phone-in show to talk about pensions. And here I was, the special guest acting as the resident pensions 'expert' for the evening. I wasn't the usual commentator on pensions for our firm, but on this occasion the first choice wasn't available so I stepped in.

As the producer started passing through some eager callers, I realized that this was just like another day at the office or out seeing clients. These were just more real people who had got themselves into a state about their money, and in particular their retirement plans. As most people do when they are starting to feel despair, they were looking for a quick fix or the easy way out.

It wasn't just those with little in the way of retirement provision who were getting worked up and calling in for our expert guidance. There were also callers with substantial sums of money in either the bank or pension funds. Retirement planning was as much of a concern for those with big pension funds as for those with only very modest savings.

In that hour-long show we experienced what I was later told was the most popular phone-in programme the station had experienced in a long time – and all on the dull topic of pensions. The only reason for this popularity was not the debut appearance of a young and nervous IFA on live radio, but the fact that the subject of pensions had hit a very raw nerve among a wide variety of people who were confused and genuinely worried about their prospects for a financially secure retirement.

Why planning for retirement matters

In your twenties, retirement seems a long way away and, hell, you might not even get there, so why worry? There always seems to be a better thing to spend your money on and many twenty-somethings question the point of putting a whole 5% or more of their precious salary away, not to be touched for 30+ years.

Then as you get older, you have the dawning realization that if you don't want to work for ever, or be penniless at 70, you need to do something about it now. And ironically, the earlier you start saving for retirement, the easier it is (even if it doesn't feel like it at 25).

There's no doubt about it, however, finding yourself at 50 with nothing in the way of saving for retirement, whether it is in the form of a pension or assets you can cash in when you retire, is not a pleasant situation to find yourself in.

If you want to avoid being in the position of most of those radio show callers, now is the time to start tackling the retirement issue. I'll make it as painless as possible. Popular pension misconceptions and a guide to getting started on retirement planning are tackled later in this chapter, but first, a quick and simple guide to how pensions work.

How do pensions work?

Since 6th April 2006 there have only really been two types of pension:

1 Defined benefit (often called 'final salary').
2 Defined contribution (sometimes called 'money purchase').

While these are both types of registered pension schemes and ultimately governed by the same 'rules', they do work in slightly different ways.

The first is the more traditional type of pension plan that was often provided by big employers. It works a bit like a promise. For every year you worked for the company you were promised a percentage of your salary when you reached a selected pension age, typically 60 or 65. Sometimes you would have to make a contribution to these plans and sometimes the employer would cover the entire cost.

If you decided to leave your employer you would hold on to the pension you had earned to date and this would become a 'deferred pension'. You wouldn't get any additional benefits added to it but they would start to pay what you had already built up when you retired.

With defined benefit pensions the focus is on the output. There is no real cash value during the life of the pension, and it is the responsibility of the company to meet the cost of providing their pension promises when you reach retirement. Your pension is expressed as an annual figure at retirement and very often this increases in line with price inflation.

The second type of pension you might come across is the defined contribution model. This is really just a pot of pension money. You and your employer pay money into the pot during your working life. Inland Revenue will also add tax relief and the money is invested, so the chances are that it will grow over time.

When you get to your chosen retirement date you have a (hopefully) big pot of money to provide an income during retirement. While there are a number of ways of converting this pot into income, the most common choice is to exchange most of the pension fund (less any tax-free cash you decide to take) for a financial instrument called an annuity. This annuity provides a guaranteed gross pension income for the rest of your life and may also include some other benefits such as death benefits for your surviving dependants. The amount of income you get from your pension depends on how much money is in your pot, your age, your life expectancy and the type of annuity benefits you decide to buy.

The main difference between these two types of pension model is that of risk. With the defined benefit pension most of the risk sits with the employer. They have made a promise to pay a certain level of pension when you reach retirement and they have to meet this financial commitment. In fact, in recent years we have seen a number of employers being unable to honour such assurances. The defined benefit or final salary pension is not a guaranteed option.

With a defined contribution pension the risk sits with you, the employee. This is because the eventual pension income your pension fund will generate depends on how much money you put into the pension pot and how much it grows by the time you reach retirement. There are some other factors that influence how much of a retirement income you will receive:

■ The charges imposed on your pension plan. High charges will erode the eventual capital value of your pension plan over time so it is important to look for low cost or, even better, high value pension plans to minimize the impact of these charges.

■ The age you decide to retire. You will receive a lower pension income if you are younger when you decide to convert your pension fund into a retirement income. This is because younger people have a longer life expectancy so the money has to last longer. If you wait until you are older, the pension income on offer will be much greater.

■ Women will get a lower pension income than men. This is because (in general) women live longer than men so the pension fund has to last longer.

■ Your health will also have an impact on your retirement income. If you are in poor health or a smoker then you may be able to get special 'enhanced' annuity rates to reflect this lower life expectancy. In fact, while smoking might have a dire impact on your personal financial planning all the way through your working life (with higher insurance premiums) it really pays off when you get to retirement age. Just make sure that you shop around for those special smoker rates – you've earned them!

■ Any benefits you add into your retirement income will reduce the starting level. For example, if you decide to provide a pension for your spouse after your death this will reduce the starting income level. Another factor that will reduce your pension income is building in escalation to keep pace with inflation. Any bells or whistles you add to your pension annuity will always have the effect of reducing the starting level of income.

The rules

Since 6th April 2006 pensions have become a lot easier to understand. The eight existing pension tax regimes were all replaced with a single set of rules for saving money for retirement in a pension. Here are 'the rules' that all pensions must follow.

■ You can contribute as much as you like and get tax relief on these contributions, within certain limits. Every man, woman and child is able to contribute up to £3,600 each tax year into a pension plan without any reference to their earnings. This means that even a baby can have a pension plan in their name and get tax relief on the contributions made on their behalf. In fact, because basic rate tax relief is added to pension contributions made by anyone, you would only have to contribute £2,808 to make a gross contribution of £3,600. The difference is added by Inland Revenue.

- If you want to contribute more than £3,600 in a tax year then you have to justify it. The absolute limit for getting tax relief on pension contributions is 100% of your earnings in a tax year. There is an upper limit on this, the Annual Allowance. For the 2006/07 tax year this annual allowance starts at £215,000, and it will increase each year. This means that you are able to put a significant amount of money into a pension plan each and every year. Under the old rules the amount of pension contributions you could make was restricted and based on your age and earnings. The new rules make life a lot easier when it comes to getting money into a pension plan.

- You cannot touch your pension fund until you get to age 50, or age 55 from 6th April 2010. The minimum retirement age for any pension is now age 50, even if it used to be higher under the old rules. This minimum age is going to be increased to 55 for all pensions from 2010.

- When you 'retire' you can take up to 25% of your pension fund as tax-free cash. In fact, under the new rules this is known as the pension commencement lump sum. The rest of your pension fund has to provide an income, but up to quarter of what you have managed to build up is available immediately as cash and under current rules is not subject to tax. It often makes sense to take this cash because if you use it to provide a pension income it becomes subject to income tax, but by investing it to produce income you may pay no tax or less tax.

- If you have a particularly large pension fund you may not be able to enjoy it all. Most people will probably not be fortunate enough to accumulate a pension fund big enough to create a tax charge, but it is something to be aware of. The new rules in April 2006 introduced a Standard Lifetime Allowance for tax privileged pension savings. In the 2006/07 tax year this starts at £1.5m. If you create a pension fund greater than this amount then the excess becomes subject to a 'recovery' charge when you take your retirement benefits. For 'recovery' read 'tax'!

Pensions aren't simple

If there is one thing I can say with certainty when talking about pensions, it is that they simply aren't simple. The Government has had an agenda for the past decade or more to 'simplify' the tax and benefit structures associated with pensions and they have introduced a number of initiatives to this end. The hope is that by making pensions easy to understand they will encourage more people to make provision for their own retirement.

You might remember two of these 'pension simplification' initiatives in particular:

■ **The day pensions were made cheap(er).** In April 2001 a new type of pension vehicle was introduced, called 'stakeholder'. In fact, stakeholder wasn't really that new, it was just a cheaper form of the existing personal pension plans that had already been around for a number of years. What made stakeholder substantially different from the old personal pension was the cost. While personal pensions could have a number of costs associated with them and no limit (other than simple marketplace competition) on the level of these charges, the humble stakeholder was only allowed one charge. By law, these pensions were only allowed to charge the investor a maximum of 1% of the value of the pension fund each year. They couldn't charge you for putting money into the pension fund, taking money out, stopping contributions, switching investment funds or doing more or less anything else within the rules. Put in the context of the existing personal pension charges this 1% charge was very cheap. However, cheap and cheerful isn't always the best value available. Very often stakeholder pensions will have a more restricted range of investment fund links than their personal pension counterparts. The real benefit that came along with the introduction of stakeholder pensions was the corresponding reduction in the cost of most personal pensions.

■ **'A-day'.** The date 6th April 2006 saw the biggest changes to pension rules for many years. A series of new rules was introduced with the aim of making pensions simpler to understand. The plan was to do away with the eight existing pension tax regimes and replace them with a single regime. This would mean that all pensions would follow the same rules. Regardless of the type of pension you could invest in the same things, have the same contribution limits and follow the same rules on what you could take out of your pension when you retired. If only it had worked this way! In reality the simplification of pensions never occurred and rather than replacing the eight existing regimes with a single rulebook, we were actually left with nine sets of rules instead.

The most common pension misconceptions

It's back to basics time. Pensions is probably the most widely misunderstood area of financial planning. To be brilliant with money you have to become brilliant with pensions.

But first, let's shatter some of those pension-related misconceptions:

1 **Pensions are bad value.** I often hear this. Sometimes it is even printed in the newspapers. Nine times out of ten the initial reaction I get from people when I bring up the subject of pensions is this statement, in one form or another. I think that the reason people think 'pensions are bad' is due to a misunderstanding of the different types of pensions and how they work. It is not unusual for people to get one type of pension mixed up with another. Sometimes they will use the 'pensions are bad' statement as an excuse for inaction.

2 Pensions are risky. Yes, they certainly can be. But remember that a pension is just a wrapper. You decide what you put inside this wrapper. This means that pensions can be as safe or as risky as you choose. With most forms of money purchase pensions (where you build up a pot of pension money) you have the ability to choose from a very wide range of investment funds. In most cases this includes cash. If you want to avoid the risk of capital loss then cash can meet this aim. As covered in the investment section on p. 124, cash might be great when it comes to avoiding capital risk, but it isn't a very good place to invest in order to beat inflation.

3 Pension planning is the same as retirement planning. This may have been the case ten or twenty years ago, but these days they are two entirely different things. Pension planning forms part of wider retirement planning, but the best advice is rarely to put all of your retirement planning eggs in one basket. The most solid retirement plans I see these days are made up of both pension and non-pension assets. They will often include property investment and ISAs working alongside traditional pension savings to build sufficient assets to fund a decent retirement.

Getting started with your own pension

If you are reading this and thinking about pensions, it probably means you either don't have a pension plan or you have one but you aren't doing much with it. Let's start by tackling the people who haven't even started a pension.

I want to make it quite clear that I am neither pro- nor anti-pension plans as such. They are simply a tool in the wider tool box of retirement planning. While advisers used to talk a lot about 'pension planning', we now talk about 'retirement planning' instead. Pensions can play a part in this retirement planning but they don't need to be the only investment vehicle used.

If you are in the position of needing to plan for your retirement then a good first port of call is normally your employer. Check to see if they have a pension scheme on offer or have plans to offer one in the near future. If your company is prepared to stick some money into a pension on your behalf then it is usually a good idea to say, 'Thank you very much' and accept it.

Even if your employer doesn't offer a pension plan where they put some money in for you, they may still be a good place to turn. Since October 2001 all employers with five or more staff (including part-time staff) have had to offer a stakeholder pension to all employees. While they don't have to pay anything into this pension on your behalf they do have to choose a suitable provider and tell you how to go about joining the scheme. If you ask them to they are legally obliged to deduct pension contributions directly from their payroll system and pay it into the stakeholder pension scheme on your behalf.

Another advantage of turning to your employer is that they will often have a professional adviser in place. Very few employers feel comfortable dealing with pension-related issues themselves so they will often outsource this task to a firm of financial advisers. You might be able to get access to this advice for free and during working hours. This certainly beats the pants off having to pay for the advice and giving up precious holiday time to talk about pensions.

But what if your company isn't enlightened when it comes to pensions? You might discover that you have to go it alone and find the advice you need by yourself. Take a look at Chapter 08 about getting professional advice. Because pensions are complex you will certainly want to use the services of an independent financial adviser (IFA) to select the right one for you. You might also want some help establishing the right level of contributions to make and deciding on an investment strategy. As a 'pension virgin' your situation should be relatively straightforward for an IFA so this shouldn't be an expensive exercise. It might even be the start of a beautiful friendship (or at least a solid, long-term professional relationship).

The alternative to having no pension is having one or more pensions to take control over. The typical client now comes to see me with no less than four existing pension plans. It's not unusual for a new client to have the details of twelve different pension arrangements in tow.

As a result of the nature of modern employment (lots of different jobs interspersed with periods of self-employment and consultancy) we appear to be getting very good at accumulating different pension arrangements. We work for a while and then take a deferred pension with us to the next employer. Rather than doing anything with the first pension we simply start a new one and leave the old one as it was. Before long we find that we are the proud owner of a collection of pension policies – all with completely different structures, investment strategies and retirement ages. In fact, we are the owner of a mess.

Taking control of this mess and understanding what we already have should be the first step for anyone with existing pension plans who wants to take a more proactive approach to their retirement planning. Without knowing what you already have it is very difficult to know what you have left to plan for.

Start by making a list of your existing pension plans. You might need to request more up-to-date information about your benefits. When asking for data make sure you ask for not only current values but also transfer values (how much you could move to a different provider) and also projections to a selected retirement age. It is often worth asking for these projections to two retirement ages, usually about five years apart. This makes it easier to understand the implications of retiring a little bit earlier or a little bit later than planned.

Once you have all of these projections you need to collate them to work out what sort of pension benefit you have already accumulated.

When you know what sort of entitlement you have already you will be able to compare it to the pension you actually want (or need) to receive when you reach your selected retirement age. The difference between these two figures is your shortfall figure that you need to plan for.

Self investment – the future of pensions?

While I hope that 'bad pensions' are a misconception in many cases, there is still a lot of ill feeling when it comes to conventional pension plans on offer from life assurance companies. Very often this comes down to a combination of factors, including the service on offer, the charges for administering the plan and managing the investments and even the performance of the investments themselves.

Investors are often disappointed with the lack of choice on offer and the quality of what they are paying for. It is said that some know the price of everything but the value of nothing, and when it comes to conventional pensions it is often the case that people know the value of what they are getting but the cost is very difficult to quantify.

A solution to this dissatisfaction may come in the form of a Self Invested Personal Pension or SIPP. These operate in a very similar way to a conventional personal pension but the difference lies in the charging structure. With a conventional personal pension there tends to be one charge to pay for everything. The cost of fund management is bundled in with the cost of actually running the pension plan and also the cost of advice.

A SIPP breaks down these charges into different areas. Instead of a single fee, a SIPP will charge you for specific services. You will pay a set-up fee and an annual fee for the running of the actual SIPP (the administration part of the service). You will pay a separate charge for the investment of the pension fund. There are also separate costs for the provision of any advice you require.

I like to think of a SIPP as being a bit like a menu-driven pension. There are certain compulsory items on the menu that you have to purchase but others are optional and you can choose to buy them if you feel the need to use them. Costs should be explicit from the outset and while a SIPP might not be as cheap as a conventional pension, it should offer better value.

Were you aware, however, that there are two different types of SIPP? For many investors the cost of a full SIPP will be prohibitive, particularly if they are not sophisticated investors and do not wish to make large pension contributions. Many people at this end of the retirement savings spectrum still want clear charges and fund choice but without the need for all the functionality of a full SIPP.

The alternative is what we call a 'hybrid' SIPP. These don't offer all of the functionality of a full SIPP, but instead allow you to access a wide range of unit-linked investment funds from a variety of fund managers. Rather than being limited to the funds of a single insurance company you are able to pick and choose between the most competitive funds available in the market. This 'fund-supermarket' approach to pension plans is likely to become more popular in the future as people demand more choice but without wanting to go as far as the expense and complexity involved with a full SIPP.

Don't forget the State

There is a great deal of debate at the moment over the future of the State pension system in the UK. Because of the profile of our ageing population there is much concern that the cost of providing the current level of State pension will not be sustainable over the longer term. There will be more older people and fewer young people in employment to support them.

Recent proposals mean that one solution to this problem is a change in the State pension age from 65 to 68 from the year 2044. This is something that younger readers need to be aware of. If you will reach 65 after 2024 then you are very likely to have an older State pension age than today's pensioners.

While the State pension system is likely to look very different in the future, you should not dismiss it entirely when putting together your retirement plan.

If you don't yet know how much you are likely to get in the way of a State pension then you should first request a free State Pension Forecast from the Pension Service. You can do this at their website at www.thepensionservice.gov.uk or by calling 0845 3000 168.

When you get your State Pension Forecast it will tell you two main things:

- The level of State pension you have already built up
- The level of State pension you are projected to receive when you reach State pension age.

Don't forget that the second figure assumes that you continue working and continue paying National Insurance contributions.

Some things you might not know about the State pension

The State pension is just as complex and confusing as pensions in general. Very few people understand how it works and the rules make it difficult to accurately predict how much pension you will receive in retirement without actually requesting a State Pension Forecast.

Here are some things that you might not know about the State pension:

- It comes in two parts – the basic State pension and an earnings-related pension (known as the State Second Pension (S2P)). Your entitlements to both parts are based on your National Insurance contributions record. The more years you work, the higher the level of State pension you accumulate.

- You automatically get five years of National Insurance credits between age 60 and age 65. This means that if you decide to stop working at age 60 you will still be treated as if you were making National Insurance contributions until you reach State pension age at 65.

- Women used to have a State pension age of 60, but this is rising to 65. From 6th April 2020 the State pension age for all women will be 65, but for women born before 5th April 1950 the pension age will still be age 60. If you were born between 1950 and 1955 you will have a State pension age somewhere between 60 and 65.

- Men need to work for 49 years and women between 44 and 49 years to get a full basic State pension. That's a long time. This means starting work at 16 and retiring at age 65. If you went to college or university this is likely to reduce your potential length of National Insurance contributions. Starting work at age 21 only gives you 44 years until age 65.

- You don't have to have a State Second Pension (S2P) from the State. If you are employed then you can choose to contract out of S2P. Instead of the State paying you this part of the State pension when you retire you can elect to receive rebates into your personal or company pension scheme instead. These rebates are invested and then you use the fund to provide you with a pension when you retire. This could be worth more or less than the S2P that was on offer. Deciding whether or not to contract out is a difficult decision which comes down to a number of factors, including the level of your earnings and how much investment risk you are prepared to take. This is certainly an area where you should seek professional independent financial advice before making a decision.

A common retirement planning mistake

The most common retirement planning mistake I see on a fairly regular basis is when a couple don't synchronize their target retirement age. This is often more of an oversight than a mistake, but it can have a devastating impact on your retirement planning all the same.

Picture this scenario. A husband and wife are age 43 and 39 respectively. They both have a target retirement age of 60, but this means very different things for each of them. For the husband this gives him a 17-year retirement planning window. His wife gets an additional four years to save for her retirement as she won't be taking the benefits for another 21 years.

But what is the reality in this case? Isn't it more likely that both the husband and wife will want to retire at the same time? Not the same age, but during the same year. It seems to me that it would be unfortunate if the husband hung up his suit for the last time on his 60th birthday but his wife had another four years of hard graft before she could enjoy their retirement together.

Well-thought-through retirement planning means working towards a target retirement date, not a target retirement age. This is another important reason for working as a team when you are completing your financial planning as a couple. The position of one spouse will inevitably affect the aims and objectives of the other.

Time to build your retirement plan

Now you know about pensions it is time to build your retirement plan. The steps are fairly straightforward:

- First work out what you already have. Find out from your pension providers what this is likely to provide you with when you retire, in terms of both tax-free cash and pension income.

- Decide when you are going to retire. The younger you are, the more difficult this will be to accurately predict. It makes sense to have a target in mind; you can always change this in the future. You might even discover that you have to change it if you're not on track to meet your retirement objectives.

- Work out how much income you will need in retirement. Base this on your current budget and work out which items you will no longer have to pay for (the mortgage, commuting, etc) and which items might actually rise during retirement (leisure costs, healthcare, household bills).

- Find out what your State pension will be. Remember that the payment of this State pension at age 65 (or later in some cases) may not coincide with your target retirement date. You might have to work out a way of bridging the gap between when you want to retire and when State pension benefits become payable.

- Now work out the difference between what you need in retirement (in terms of income) and what you already have in place. This is your retirement shortfall figure and represents the income you need to create between now and your target retirement date.

- Put in place a retirement plan to hit this shortfall figure. This might involve pensions or you might choose to use non-pension assets. Either way, get projections based on a number of different contribution levels to ensure that you are putting enough money aside today to meet your targets in the future.

- Rinse and repeat. This is not an exercise to do once and then forget about. Put a date in your diary to review your retirement plan each and every year. It should only take a couple of hours but these are probably the most valuable couple of hours of your life. Having sufficient income in retirement makes the difference between living in comfort and living in poverty. You are in a position to take control – so do it!

KEY POINTS

1 Retirement planning and pensions are the long-term part of the Money Tree, and everyone needs to take personal responsibility for ensuring they have a financially secure retirement. Nobody else is going to look after you in your old age.

2 There are two types of pensions – those that promise a final benefit and those where you build up a pot of money that you later convert into an income.

3 Since 6th April 2006 the rules associated with pensions have changed a lot and there is now a single set of rules that applies to all types of pensions. Understand the main rules and you will understand how all pensions work.

4 Common misconceptions about pensions are often an excuse for inaction. Think in terms of retirement planning rather than pensions planning, with pensions playing a part in your wider financial plan. Not all pensions are bad. Misunderstood pensions are often thought of as bad value.

5 The future of pensions appears to be self-investment and SIPPs, but only if you need or want this additional functionality. The ability to self-invest comes at a price so if you don't want this there are alternative types of pension plans to consider that still give you access to a wide range of investment funds.

6 The State will probably provide a pension benefit for you in retirement, and you should take this into account when drawing up your retirement plans. Be aware that the State pension system is subject to change and you should regularly review how these changes might impact upon your own plans.

7 Now is the time to build your retirement plan. The longer you leave your retirement planning, the harder it becomes as it costs more to fund a shorter term to retirement. Retirement planning is cheaper if you start early because your money is invested for longer and has the potential for better returns.

Time for advice

Advice is what we ask for when we already know the answer but wish we didn't.

Erica Jong (1942–)

08

The knowledge you have gained from reading this book will put you in a really strong position to take control of your finances. It should also mean that you can understand the advice provided by professionals and challenge it where necessary.

Using a professional adviser is not always necessary. If you are prepared to do a lot of research and to take the responsibility for your financial choices, then you can survive without their services. However, many people find that they lack the time, inclination or knowledge (and often all three) to effectively manage their own financial planning.

This chapter of *The Money Tree* explores the types of professional advisers you might encounter and what to expect from them. Getting your working relationship with a professional adviser right is part of maintaining a strong and healthy Money Tree.

There are three main types of adviser you might need to work with when planning your finances:

1 Financial advisers

2 Accountants

3 Solicitors.

Each of these professionals has a different role to play in the development of your Money Tree. Some people will not require the services of all of them, and you might only need to choose an adviser at different stages during your life.

Whenever you speak to a professional adviser, be it for financial advice or some other service, you should be very clear about your objective for seeking the advice. Are you looking for tactical, short-term help with one or two aspects of your financial life or more strategic input about longer-term plans?

Different advisers will offer different services to their clients, and one who is very good with tactical matters might not be the best choice for a more holistic planning-based relationship.

Different advisers serve different purposes

When you are looking for professional guidance on your personal finances you might need to work with a particular type of adviser depending on the area of advice. In some cases you might need to work with more than one type of adviser at the same time.

Below are some common examples of different areas of financial advice and the professional adviser (or advisers) you might consider working with.

Retirement planning

As well as seeking counsel from an independent financial adviser you might also want to work closely with your accountant, particularly if you are self-employed or a director of a limited company. The most efficient way of making pension contributions (and the maximum allowable contributions) can often be a complex calculation if you fall into one of these two categories. There might also be issues about capital gains tax (CGT) on the eventual sale of your business to consider.

Inheritance tax and estate planning

This is a time when it is essential to work closely with both an independent financial adviser and a solicitor. Trying to establish the most appropriate way to structure your estate (including the family home) for inheritance tax purposes can involve making some very difficult decisions about giving up immediate control of certain assets. A solicitor must be consulted for their specialist knowledge of tax and trusts.

Mortgage advice

In most cases you can make do with just working with your independent financial adviser (assuming they offer mortgage advice) or an independent mortgage adviser. There is also a need for a conveyancer during the process of house sale and/or purchase. For simple transactions your IFA or mortgage adviser might suggest using an online conveyancing service where you can monitor the progress of the case at any time of the day. The need for a traditional solicitor has really diminished in these cases and you can often save a great deal of time (and money) by making use of the services of an online conveyancer.

Many people shop around for their own mortgage and with the availability of online comparison websites this is an attractive option. Choosing a mortgage should never be done on rates alone, so the services of a professional adviser in this area is important. Also bear in mind that mortgage advisers will often have access to rates and deals that the general public are not offered directly.

The professional adviser power meeting

I've now managed to get some of my clients into the habit of arranging joint meetings not just with me, as their IFA, but also with their accountant and/or solicitor. I call this the 'professional adviser power meeting'. This approach makes sense for a number of reasons:

■ It means that each adviser is working towards the same objective. I've seen so many occasions when each adviser is pulling in a different direction and trying (unintentionally in most cases) to undo a lot of the good work done by another. Working as a team is bound to get better results and ensure that everyone is focused on achieving the same goal for you, the client.

■ Each adviser is likely to have a different area of expertise and bringing these together can only benefit the client. The implications of advice might not be immediately apparent to, for example, your accountant, but with everyone in the same room at the same time you stand a much better chance of filling in all the gaps – financial, taxation and legal.

■ Everyone will know something different about a client. I know a lot of clients who will tell their solicitor one set of information and their financial adviser another. They don't intend to mislead anyone and in most cases this is just the unintended consequence of different questions being asked by different professionals. Having all three advisers in the same meeting will ensure that they are giving their recommendations based on the same understanding of your current position and financial objectives.

Be warned, this 'professional adviser power meeting' approach can sometimes prove to be expensive. The cost of having three professional advisers in the same building at the same time can sometimes outweigh the benefit of bringing them all together.

What you should always ensure happens is that each of your advisers copies the others in on any important correspondence (about changes to advice or new recommendations). This at least means that your other advisers are aware of what changes are taking place and, if necessary, they can flag up any concerns or observations they might have.

To put this into effect you will need to tell each adviser who the other professionals you work with are and how to contact them. In many cases you will also need to give them a written instruction to release this sort of confidential information to those people.

If this happened more often then I am convinced that fewer advisory-related mistakes would take place. It's not about putting your advisers in the position where they scrutinize each other's every word, but instead making sure that a high level of awareness is maintained between your professional adviser team.

So much choice

When you go searching for a financial adviser you will be faced with a wide range of choices. Since June 2005 the services of a financial adviser have been 'depolarized'. To understand what this means for you it is important to explain the way things used to work before this new regime was introduced.

In the 'good old days' there were only two types of financial adviser – they were either tied or independent.

The tied adviser would represent one company and one company only. This type of adviser was only allowed to sell products from the company they worked for or represented. This rarely offered best value for their customers. It is fair to assume that no single company can consistently be the most competitive provider of every financial product.

The more popular alternative to tied advice was the independent financial adviser. This type of adviser didn't have any ties or vested interests in a particular product provider. In fact, they acted in the interests of their customer rather than a single company.

While independent financial advice was always the logical choice it was still the case that people would seek advice from tied advisers. This was often down to the way these services were advertised or the leveraging of existing relationships with banks or building societies.

The ways things work today is slightly different. Under current rules an adviser is able to be:

- Tied.
- Multi-tied. This means that they can only sell you products from a limited range of providers. This type of adviser cannot claim to be independent because of their restricted access to the market
- Whole of market. This type of adviser is almost an IFA, but they rely entirely on commission from selling you products and do not offer the option to pay a fee for their advice instead
- Independent (IFA). As well as having access to the whole of the market this type of financial adviser always offers you the choice of paying a fee for their services (rather than receiving a commission on sales).

How to find a financial adviser

Just how do you go about finding a financial adviser? The best way is by personal referral. If a friend, family member or work colleague has had a positive experience of an adviser, this is a great place to start. The fact that your friend has experienced good advice and service is a fairly sound indicator that you should experience the same.

But what if nobody you know can make a recommendation? Your contacts may not know any financial advisers. Maybe they do but are not impressed with what these people have to offer. Maybe they want to keep them all to themselves!

If you are stuck for an introduction then there are still plenty of places to turn. The internet offers a number of online directories where financial advisers are listed, along with details of their areas of expertise.

My favourite three directories for finding a financial adviser are:

- **www.unbiased.co.uk** – this is a website run by IFA Promotion, an industry body responsible for promoting independent financial advice.

To use this website you simply enter your postcode and click 'find an IFA'. It is also possible to filter advisers by the specialist area you want to discuss. Results are then listed by the distance of the adviser to your postcode. This website offers you a voucher to print out and take with you to your first meeting for a free consultation. Most IFAs will offer their first meeting without charge or obligation anyway, but this voucher does give you some comfort that you will not be charged for that first encounter with a new IFA.

- **www.thepfs.co.uk** – the Personal Finance Society is a professional body for financial advisers and they offer a 'Find an Adviser' service on their website. If you are seeking advice on a more complex area of financial planning then this is probably the best directory to make use of. You can filter the results by the area of advice you are seeking or elect to view only chartered financial planners, those with the highest level of professional qualification. It is also possible to choose whether you would like to meet with a male or female adviser.

- **www.advisermap.co.uk** – this website is an innovative new online adviser directory that places professional advisers (not just IFAs) on a searchable map of the UK. By integrating their directory with Google Map technology it is possible to explore the map and find a local adviser with a click of the mouse rather than typing in lots of information. This website is a great way of finding not only a financial adviser but also a mortgage consultant, accountant or solicitor. It even displays a set of directions to your first consultation.

A question of qualifications and regulation

You can (and should) check that your financial adviser is authorized and regulated by the Financial Services Authority (FSA). You can check this online at www.fsa.gov.uk/register. In order to be an authorized and regulated financial adviser in the UK it is necessary to have passed a certain exam. This entry-level qualification is the Certificate in Financial Planning (CFP) and is issued by the Chartered Insurance Institute. It used to be called the Financial Planning Certificate (FPC).

Be warned that this certificate is nothing to write home about. In terms of comparison to other qualifications it is probably somewhere between GCSE and A level. An adviser with the CFP can demonstrate a very basic level of competence in the provision of financial advice but this is inadequate when it comes to more demanding or complex areas.

If you are looking for a financial adviser then always make sure that they hold the Advanced Financial Planning Certificate (AFPC). This is a much more challenging set of qualifications that are made up of modules equivalent to degree level. To pass the AFPC requires a serious level of study and commitment.

Certain elements of the AFPC exam become more important if you are seeking financial advice on specific areas of your Money Tree. If you want information on pensions then make sure your adviser holds the 'G60: Pensions' qualification. If you need to talk about inheritance tax and estate planning then the qualification to look out for is called 'G10: Taxation and Trusts'. A business seeking advice on how best to protect its key people would want to find an adviser with 'G30: Business Financial Planning'.

Do not be afraid to ask your adviser about their qualifications. While experience plays an important part in the advice process it should always be backed up by relevant professional credentials. There is no substitute for the adviser having invested their own time in studying for higher level exams. Basic qualifications are all very well for basic advice, but in my own experience it is very rare for anyone to only require basic advice!

There are two main qualifications higher than the Advanced Financial Planning Certificate.

The first is the Certified Financial Planner (CFP) licence. This involves completing a case study or examination to demonstrate the ability to construct a holistic financial plan that meets a number of rigorous standards. If you are looking for comprehensive advice about your financial planning then look for a CFP holder. Be aware that someone with this qualification is likely to be more expensive than an adviser without it.

The latest higher level professional qualification for financial advisers is that of Chartered Financial Planner. This has only been available for a relatively short period of time so the number of Chartered Planners is still limited, but it really does represent the top level of the profession. Once again, expect to pay a premium for advice from somebody who holds this qualification.

Top Tips for a healthy relationship with a financial adviser

If you want to build a long and successful relationship with a financial adviser there are a few points you should keep in mind.

1 Find the right adviser in the first place

Your chances of a successful long-term relationship with a financial adviser will be much higher if you start by choosing the best adviser for you. Do some research and meet more than one adviser to find the one that best fits your requirements. This investment of your time at the start of the process will pay dividends later if it means that you can stick with the same adviser for a long time.

2 Be open and honest

A financial adviser will need to know everything about you, in terms of your current financial position and future financial objectives. Failing to disclose information in the early stage of your relationship could have a negative impact on the quality of advice the adviser is able to provide. Remember that they will make recommendations based on their understanding of your position and objectives. If either of these two areas is unclear it could have a detrimental effect on the counsel they give.

3 Establish what you need and want

If you only need help with one or maybe two areas of your financial life then make this very clear to the adviser. They may still need to find out about all areas of your finances. This is because there is a crossover when it comes to financial planning and different areas of your current position may have an impact on the advice they give. Setting the boundaries at any early stage will also reduce the chances of you becoming a sales victim, as the adviser will be limited in their scope of guidance. They may well still try to offer you advice on other areas of your life and it is up to you to decide whether or not to give them the opportunity to provide it.

4 Find out what ongoing relationship you will have

Ask this question at the start of the process with your new financial adviser. Some will expect to provide advice and then have no ongoing relationship; you will become a customer rather than a client. Others will want to seek an ongoing relationship. Remember that there is likely to be a cost associated with this relationship, particularly if you want a proactive annual review service.

There is no such thing as a free lunch

For many years the services of a financial adviser were considered free of charge. Because money rarely changed hands it was difficult to see the real cost of advice. But there is no such thing as a free lunch and there is certainly no such thing as free financial advice. The reason that these financial advisers could apparently operate more akin to a charity than a business was the commission they received.

For every product, policy or investment sold the product provider or fund manager pays a healthy commission to the adviser. By law, this commission is always disclosed to the customer before the sale takes place, but this is very often hard to understand in the context of a transaction.

Times are changing when it comes to payment for advice. With the charges associated with some financial products falling, there is now less of a profit margin available for the product providers to pay commissions to the financial salespeople who promote them. The world of financial services is starting to realize that commission has a limited shelf-life.

The alternative to paying for advice through commission is to pay a fee. This might be charged as a project fee for an agreed activity or as an hourly rate for advice and other services provided. Paying a fee has some advantages when compared to the traditional commission route. For a start it is much more explicit. You can see exactly what it is you are paying which should make it easier to understand what value you are getting for your money. Secondly, paying a fee breaks the link between the adviser and the product. It means that they do not need to recommend a financial product in order to be paid for their services. Sometimes a product is not the most suitable solution to a financial problem so the payment of a fee for advice removes the temptation to recommend it regardless of real need.

Shopping around for your professional adviser on price alone is a foolish activity. What really matters, when paying for any service, is value. Whether you are paying for financial advice by fee or through commission (you are paying for the advice either way), you have to be satisfied that you are getting good value for your money.

What to expect from your first meeting

Every financial adviser is slightly different, so no two first meetings will be exactly the same. All advisers are, however, expected to follow certain rules and requirements, which means that there are certain common elements to anticipate. By knowing what to look out for you will be able to ask the right questions and get much more value out of this encounter.

The following is a brief summary of a typical first meeting I would typically have with a new client.

- The meeting might take place at my offices or at the client's home or place of work. I know that different advisers have different policies when it comes to this. Some will only meet with clients at their own offices. This is to reduce valuable travelling time and also to get the new client to show some commitment to the advice process. I tend to be more relaxed when it comes to the meeting venue. The only important factor to me is that the environment is appropriate for a meeting where confidential facts and figures are likely to be discussed. An open-plan office or busy café doesn't always make a good venue for your first meeting with a financial adviser.

- There is some paperwork that the adviser should start by presenting. This forms part of their regulatory requirement to disclose their status and the way they do business with clients. You should be given three main documents at a very early stage in the first meeting. These are:

  - Terms of Business Letter. This is typically a two-page letter that sets out the way the adviser does business. It should explain their status (independent, tied or other) and any protection you receive by virtue of dealing with them as a financial adviser. They will ask you to sign one copy of this document to prove that you have seen it and also give you a copy for your records.

  - Key Facts about Our Services. This document became a legal requirement in June 2005 when the Financial Services Authority (FSA) decided that clients should be able to see at a glance who they were dealing with. This is supposed to aid the process of shopping around for different advisers.

  - Key Facts about the Costs of Our Services. This is another FSA mandatory document that explains the typical costs of using the adviser and the methods of payment available to you. Your adviser may charge commission, fees or a combination of the two. If they charge for their advice through commission then they are obliged to show a comparison table in this document that sets out the maximum commission they will take for a particular product versus the market average commission. This table really does aid the process of shopping around so make sure you are given a copy at an early stage and hang on to this for your records.

If the adviser charges fees and does not offer a commission option then they will not show this comparison table. However, they will explain the typical fees they might charge a client.

■ The next part of the first meeting is known as 'fact-finding'. This is likely to take up the majority of the meeting and it will involve the adviser asking you lots of questions about your current position and future objectives. The more information you can give them at this stage, the better. In fact, there is no advantage to holding back any information. Some of the questions you are asked (for example, about your health) may seem irrelevant and very personal but the answers can have a big impact on the advice that is provided. Go to the meeting armed with the answers to the questions you are likely to be faced with. When I arrange to see new clients I always send them a copy of my financial questionnaire ahead of the meeting to give them the chance to see what sort of information they will need.

■ You should use the first meeting as an opportunity to ask the adviser a lot about their qualifications, experience, charges and general way of doing things. Do not be afraid to dig deeply and ask searching questions. No financial adviser should shy away from giving you full and honest answers to any relevant questions you pose.

■ The adviser will typically finish the meeting by explaining what happens next. It could be the case that they will need to go away to do some research before presenting you with a recommendation (if they work on a commission basis). If they are a professional fee-charging adviser then they will probably write to you with a proposal for their services that will also set out the fees involved. Once you have accepted this proposal they will begin to construct a recommendation.

One thing is certain when it comes to the first meeting with a financial adviser – they should probably not be providing you with any specific advice. It takes time to construct a recommendation and professional financial advice is not something to be rushed.

KEY POINTS

1 When the time comes to seek professional advice about your money you may need one or more of three main types of adviser – financial advisers, accountants and solicitors.

2 Each type of professional adviser will have a different role to play. In certain areas of your financial planning you may need to involve more than one type of adviser at the same time, and this can require careful coordination to ensure that everyone is working towards the same goal.

3 A financial adviser can either be independent, whole of market, multi-tied or tied. The only way to ensure that you get access to advice on every product in the market and the option to pay a fee is by working with an independent financial adviser (IFA).

4 Finding a financial adviser can be tough. If you cannot find one by personal recommendation then there are online directories available to make your job easier.

5 Don't be afraid to ask a financial adviser about their qualifications to ensure that they have sufficient knowledge to deal with the type of advice you require. A basic professional qualification is only any good if you need basic advice. Seek advice from an IFA who holds at least the Advanced Financial Planning Certificate (AFPC).

6 There is a cost for advice and you pay for it either through commissions or fees. In order to get complete impartiality and ensure that the adviser does not have an incentive to sell you a financial product you should pay fees for three different services – advice, implementation and review.

7 Every first meeting with an adviser will be slightly different but most will follow the same general format. Expect to answer lots of questions about your finances and your goals. Go to the meeting prepared and remember to ask the adviser questions about their qualifications, experience and way of working.

Bringing it all together

> All you need is the plan, the road map, and the courage to press on to your destination.
>
> Earl Nightingale (1922–1989)

09

This book has covered a lot of ground. Each chapter put you in a position where you could make important decisions about that particular area of your financial life. Now it is time to take a more strategic, longer-term view of your Money Tree. This chapter will show you how to take what you have learnt and build your financial plan.

There are two ways of dealing with your personal financial planning. You can choose to amble through life, making *ad hoc* decisions as and when you need to. This is reactive financial planning and it is the way that most people tend to deal with their Money Tree; they will only address their personal financial planning when a life event (marriage, unemployment, death, etc) forces them to do so.

The other option is to take a more proactive stance. Rather than allowing your money to control you, plan how you can control your money. Planning in advance of life events means that you have greater control. Because money can also influence our emotions this approach should lead to you being much happier as well.

How to build a financial plan

Building your financial plan is all about these three key questions:

1 Where are you now?

2 Where would you like to be?

3 How are you going to get there?

Where are you now?

The first question should be relatively easy to answer, but many people are still living like an ostrich with their head buried in the sand. Working out your current financial position means setting aside a couple of hours of quiet time and arming yourself with recent statements and a single sheet of paper or a spreadsheet to summarize the whole lot in one place.

Just because it is easy, from a practical point of view, to work out your current financial position doesn't necessarily make it an enjoyable task. Deciding to take this first step often means facing up to debt demons and uncertainty that you have been trying your best to avoid. In fact, completing this exercise can be the most challenging step in the financial planning process for many people.

I can promise that you will feel better as soon as you complete this task. If you are the sort of person who has been avoiding confrontation with your financial paperwork, then knowing exactly where you stand will take a great deal of weight from your shoulders. You might not be happy with the facts and figures laid out in front of you but you will be proud of yourself for taking this brave first step.

But realistically, how do you go about collating the information you need to complete this first step? Different strategies will work for different people. It is best to find a strategy that works for you and then stick to it.

The way that I carry out this 'personal financial audit' is to get a ring binder with twenty or so different file dividers. On the front of each file divider I write the name of a particular bank account, savings account, investment or policy. I'm a big believer in keeping things simple so twenty file dividers are more than enough to cover all of my financial arrangements. For some of the clients

I start to work with this is barely enough to cover their pension plans alone! I've worked with people where three or four large ring binders have been put together during this first stage of the planning process.

Group your latest statements and valuations together in a logical order within your ring binder. Why not use the chapters in this book to build a file structure?

- Debt – credit card and store card statements, personal loans, credit agreements
- Tax – any correspondence from HM Revenue & Customs
- Savings – the latest statements from your bank or building society savings accounts
- Mortgage – your latest mortgage statement
- Protection – life assurance and other protection policy documents
- Investments – current valuations of your investments (including ISAs)
- Pensions – current valuations of your pension plans and projections to your selected retirement age
- Advisers – the latest financial plan or advice letter from your financial adviser (if you have one)

Once you have put all of this information in one place it is time to summarize. This saves you the time and effort of sorting through hundreds of pages of information to find the key facts and figures. At the front of my 'personal financial audit' ring binder I keep a couple of sheets of paper with this summary. It's a printout from a spreadsheet I keep on my computer which means that I can update the figures without having to rewrite the whole thing each time. I try to update this once a month so that I always have the most recent values at a glance. It is also updated if something big changes, like selling an investment or increasing the level of life cover on a policy.

As well as policy and account values you should also make a note here of some other key facts and figures:

- If you own your house then make a note of the current value of your property. It is virtually impossible to know its exact value until you actually sell it, but take a best guess based on how much other similar properties have sold for during the past twelve months or so.

- Write down details of your earnings as both an annual figure before tax and the net amount (after tax) you get paid each month.

- Make a note of any unusual expenditure or income that you know might arise in the future. In terms of expenditure this might include the cost of a holiday or any home improvements you have planned. Unusual income includes an annual bonus or an inheritance.

Where would you like to be?

Once you know where you are the next step in building your financial plan is to work out where you want to be. Think of your financial plan like driving directions: before you can work out the best route on a map you have to know both where you are starting from and where you want to get to.

What you need at this stage is a degree of certainty. Using ball-park figures to build your financial plan is fine, but you have to accept that this will lead to a less useful strategy. It is understandable that you might not, for example, know exactly when you plan to retire. For most people this date is a long way in the future. However, giving some thought to this sort of timing and then setting a notional date really helps you build a financial plan that will work. Just because you decide to retire at, say, 65 doesn't commit you to that as your actual retirement date.

It does give you a definite date in the future so you can fine-tune any plans you put in place.

List your financial objectives under three headings:

- Short term – anything you want to achieve within the next five years
- Medium term – your financial goals within five to ten years
- Long term – the stuff you want to get done in ten years or longer.

These financial goals and objectives should include absolutely anything that is connected with money. Here is an example:

Short term

- Pay off my credit cards
- Starting saving some money
- Review my mortgage to make sure I'm not paying too much.

Medium term

- Move to a new house with a bit more space for our growing family.

Long term

- Repay my mortgage
- Have enough money in my pension to retire.

The financial plan in this example is good, but it could be a lot better. Making these objectives SMART will do a great deal towards improving your likelihood of success. SMART stands for:

- Specific
- Measurable

- Achievable or Attainable
- Realistic
- Timely.

What this means is that for each item on your list you should be able to place a tick against most of the SMART points. A better version of the financial plan from this example might be:

Short term

- Pay off my ABC and XYZ credit card completely, within the next five months, by moving them both to a nil interest rate balance transfer credit card and repaying one-fifth of the balance off each month from my surplus monthly income. My target is to receive a credit card statement in six months' time showing a nil balance.
- Starting saving some money. As soon as I have paid off my credit card debt I will redirect my surplus monthly income into a savings account. I will use the internet to research the most competitive interest rates and set up a direct debit to ensure that I commit to saving this amount each month.
- Review my mortgage to make sure I'm not paying too much. Within the next month I will meet with an independent mortgage adviser and ask them to review my current mortgage deal with a view to saving me money. I will use the money I save to boost the value of my savings each month.

Medium term

- Move to a new house with a bit more space for our growing family. In six years' time we plan to move to a new house with two extra bedrooms to accommodate the children we plan to have. In four years' and six months' time we will begin visiting estate agents to determine our ideal home and also review our financial plan to ensure that we can afford the house we want.

Long term

■ Repay my mortgage by the time I reach my 50th birthday so I can use the money I am spending on this to pay for my children's education and also maximize my pension contributions. When I meet the independent mortgage adviser (within the next month) to review my existing mortgage deal I will discuss the best strategy for making sure that my mortgage is repaid in time for my 50th birthday.

■ Have enough money in my pension to retire. I would like to retire when I reach my 60th birthday on a pension income equivalent to two-thirds of my current salary (adjusted for inflation between now and retirement). I will find out how much I would need to contribute to a pension to reach this target, taking investment growth and charges into account. I will also review my pension values at the end of each year to ensure that I remain on track to reach this goal.

Do you agree that this financial plan is much better than the plan in the first example? It contains all of the same goals but with a little more detail they become much more effective than before. Rather than being stated as vague financial objectives the goals are being stated with certainty.

At this stage it is important to check that your objectives are all realistic. Setting unrealistic goals and objectives is a short cut to failure and disappointment. Not only will you fail to reach your targets but you will be left feeling disheartened about the whole financial planning process. By sticking to realistic objectives you stand a much greater chance of success. You might want to retire at 30 but if you don't have the means to support your lifestyle in retirement then this is not a reasonable goal. There is little point in building a financial plan that is going to lead to failure.

How are you going to get there?

Now that you know where you are starting from and where you want to go, it is time to work out how you are going to get there. Getting from A to B when you are driving a car is usually pretty straightforward, with the exception of unexpected roadworks or traffic jams. You either know where you are going because the route is familiar to you or you don't know the area well so you use a map or driving directions from someone else.

Building a financial plan is just like planning a driving route. You either know your way from where you are now to where you want to go or you have to use a map to get there. The contents of this book can form part of your financial planning directions. They will give you a broad foundation in each of the main areas of your financial planning.

Start by prioritizing each of your financial objectives. It may not be possible to achieve each and every one of them. Sometimes you just have to accept that you can only afford the most pressing financial concerns. It can often be difficult to work out which financial objective should take priority over the others. This is a very personal decision to make and only you will know which is the most important to you. The best way to work this out is to think about the potential impact of not meeting that particular objective. It might be the case that the worst outcome from failure to meet an objective means it is your most important financial priority.

After prioritizing your objectives you have to draw up your battle plan. How exactly are you going to get there? Because you have made each of your financial objectives SMART, this stage in the planning process should be relatively straightforward. Decide how much of your resources you can allocate to each objective.

Once you have a battle plan in place you must commit it to paper. Trying to run a financial plan from memory is a dangerous game. Because you are juggling multiple financial objectives it is inevitable that you will forget one or two of them from time to time. Getting a financial plan down on paper also makes it more likely that you will actually follow it. Keep your plan in a safe place, because it contains confidential information, but don't put it away somewhere it will never see the light of day again!

Constructing your financial plan isn't where it ends. It is not enough to simply write a plan and then forget about it. In the first year I suggest that you review it once every three months. You can move this to once every six months in year two and then annually from the third year onwards.

A review of your financial plan means following a very similar process to actually building it in the first place:

- Work out where you are
- Check that you still want to reach the same financial objectives
- Ensure that your steps to get from A to B don't need to change.

Write down the details of each review on a new page and, crucially, don't throw away your original plan. Even though your financial objectives will change a lot over time it is important to keep your original plan and details of each review so that you can monitor these changes. When you look back at your original plan after five or ten years you will be amazed how much has altered!

If you want your Money Tree to prosper, it will. Giving adequate time and attention to the growth of your Money Tree will lead to greater wealth, more security and (ultimately) financial happiness.

KEY POINTS

1 You have two choices when it comes to growing your Money Tree – either react to life events or take a proactive stance and plan for them. You choose either to let your money control you or to control it yourself.

2 Start building a financial plan by working out where you are now. This can be a scary task for some people but it is worthwhile. The best way to work out your current financial position is to be incredibly organized.

3 Decide where you want to get to. Write down your financial objectives and make sure they are SMART. If your financial objectives are detailed they stand a greater chance of success.

4 Work out how you are going to get there by prioritizing your objectives and writing down a strategy for reaching each one.

5 Don't forget about your financial plan! Review your progress every three months in year one, every six months in year two and then annually. Keep hold of your original financial plan so you can see how much your objectives change over time.

INDEX